MW01061374

SUCCESS
THROUGH
MIND POWER

*How to Be a Winner
in The Game of Life*

ROY HUNTER

Westwood Publishing Company, Inc.

© 1986 Roy Hunter. All rights reserved

Published by
Westwood Publishing Company, Inc.
312 Riverdale Drive
Glendale, CA 91204

ISBN 0-930298-27-6

Printed in the United States of America

Acknowledgments

My inspiration for this book is my mentor and teacher Charles Tebbetts, who through his teaching and personal example convinced me that the power of the mind is the greatest power in the world.

I am also indebted to Gil Boyne, the man who trained Charles Tebbetts and whose unique philosophy and understanding of Mind Power constitute the essence of this work.

Preface

Success motivation seminars attract millions of dollars invested by people desiring to improve their lives. The same people frequently feel frustrated, however, when they find themselves unable to apply what has obviously worked for others.

A friend of mine, a former insurance agent, voiced the feelings of many by asking: "If this works for other people, why can't I make it work for *me*?"

That is a valid question deserving a valid answer.

The fact is, it *can* work for you—and the purpose of this book is to show you how!

Contents

Contents

Session Four
Putting It Together

Appendix I

Appendix II

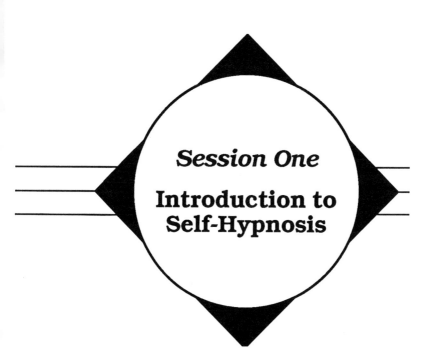

Session One

**Introduction to
Self-Hypnosis**

Chapter 1

Introduction

My clients frequently ask me why they find themselves unable to accomplish seemingly simple goals and objectives through willpower. My response is to explain that accepting *any* new habit pattern requires subconscious cooperation—otherwise your conscious decision to make the change is undermined by your own subconscious belief in failure.

There is a basic law of the mind at work:

Whenever your conscious and subconscious are in conflict, your subconscious invariably wins!

This has been proven repeatedly: by smokers unable to stop without outside help, by outgoing people suddenly finding themselves petrified with fright when speaking in public, and by each of us as we wonder why things we *want* to change do not come easily.

Since hypnosis is an effective way to facilitate change at a subconscious level, there is increasing interest today in the benefits of hypnosis and self-hypnosis.

Self-hypnosis helped me so much in changing my own life that I feel compelled to share the secret of *how* to change with those who are ready to accept it. I also believe in the win/win philosophy, so I teach people both in private and group sessions things that I feel can help them do more than what they paid me for in the first place.

Clients frequently leave my office with a new skill that will help them attain many personal goals beyond those addressed in the actual sessions. This skill is what I call **Mind Power Exercise**. In simple terms, **Mind Power Exercise** means the correct combination of self-hypnosis, creative daydreaming, and proper use of affirmations for attaining goals in life, whether they be personal or professional.

Mind Power Exercise is a mental exercise enabling you to take better control of your own life!

I realize that there are numerous self-help books on the market already. The problem, however, is that we find a piece here and a piece there, like pieces of a jigsaw puzzle—and we battle with the subconscious for acceptance of the pieces. What I teach is not really new—it is a way of putting together information that is already available—but putting it together in a way that really works.

Subconscious Resistance to Change

All our present habits, mannerisms, and thought patterns are the results of past subconscious "programming" from parents, teachers, peers, coworkers, television—a variety of sources. This programming can either propel us into success against all odds—or keep us from it. In order to succeed, then, it becomes vitally important for us to learn how to take charge of our *own* subconscious programming.

And in order to take charge of your own programming, your subconscious must be persuaded, not forced, to help you succeed. Unless you incorporate a success technique into your own *subconscious* mind, you can be defeated by your subconscious resistance to change.

Virtually all of us have experienced the difficulty of changing a habit pattern at one time or another. Once your subconscious learns something, it does not like to change; and the more you try to force the change, the greater the resistance. However, from the countless self-help books on the market and the millions of dollars invested annually by salespeople alone for motivational seminars, it is obvious that people— at least consciously— are ready for change! And if *you* are among this group, this book is for you!

Accepting Responsibility

I was one of the many who used to find frustration reading excellent books that worked for others but did not seem to work well for me. My conscious mind totally accepted the ideas. I even used affirmations too numerous to count— and it seemed like things got worse. A typical response one seeking success hears from one who has already found it is, "Whatever you believe, you can achieve." Of course, some will go on to expound that if you think positively you get positive results— or that you get exactly what you "program" for in life. I desired earnestly to change the program, but my subconscious resisted.

Somehow I felt that I had the ability to succeed. *With my intellect I believed this.* I had already succeeded in business for several years— even though not to my fullest expectations— yet now found myself unable to make things work that had worked before. Certainly there were "extenuating circumstances"— or rather, excuses made up by my mind to justify subconscious beliefs so that it was now permissible to fail. It would have been too devastating to my self-image to admit to myself that I had now programmed myself for failure as I was told.

For me, the first step was *accepting responsibility for where I was in life!* This was difficult at best— especially with some other personal difficulties that I was also experiencing at the time and perceiving as failures. Now it was time to let go of the past and change the present. It was a difficult process at first because of subconscious resistance; and those who were telling me to "change the program" could not tell me *how* to change the program! It's easy to think positive when your life is already full of positive things—but how do you go from negative thinking to positive thinking when your life is full of negatives?

"Old Tapes" Must Be Changed

In my business, we refer to all this subconscious "programming" as "old tapes," since our minds retain everything, just like a computer. But unfortunately, we can't just *erase* a program tape, we have to record a new program over it.

All old tapes aren't bad. Most of us are "programmed" not to cross the street when there are cars coming, to say "thank you" when appropriate, to act according to certain social standards. We accept these tapes every day without thinking about them. But we also subconsciously accept old tapes such as "no one in my family was ever rich" or "I'm too dumb to learn algebra" or "all my relatives are heavy, it runs in the family."

When the subconscious mind is full of negative program tapes, it's virtually impossible to stay in a positive frame of mind unless those tapes are changed on a subconscious level.

The trick is to be aware of and *choose* which tapes you wish to accept and which you wish to "record over" or change.

Many salespeople with excellent ability have imagined losing a sale during a slump—only to see another sale "bomb off" again as usual. What makes matters worse is that a business slump sometimes becomes self-perpetuating. The negative result reinforces the subconscious belief that business is slow, so we can subconsciously do self-defeating things—even while going through all the right mechanics to produce new business.

A person desiring to take off weight can go on a very sophisticated program of weight control, but unless the *subconscious* is changed, the conscious change in behavior is only temporary.

What is needed, then, is a simple way of creating *new program tapes* in the subconscious mind—and the *subconscious* must accept them in order for the changes to last. I have taught numerous business people the formula in my "Success" seminars—and my objective now is to put the same seminar in book form.

How to Use This Book

Mind Power Exercise is divided into four sessions, just as I teach them, to make it easier for you to apply the material presented. You may skim through this entire book at one sitting. In fact, I hope it grabs your interest enough to want to do so! However, you will derive maximum benefit from the material by investing yourself in at least four self-help sessions at separate times.

Also be sure to take time to do the self-hypnosis exercises outlined at the end of each session. If you do, you can gain skills that will last you a lifetime and which are applicable to many areas of your life. If you don't, you may have just one more "dust collector" in your library.

This book *is* different—because it is not intended to tell you *what* to change in your life, but to teach you *how* to change. You select your own goals and paths, then use *Mind Power Exercise* for success!

Chapter 2

What Is Hypnosis?

The word hypnosis, coined by an English physician in the 19th century, has given us an inaccurate picture for over 100 years—it is derived from the Greek word *hypnos*, meaning sleep. But hypnosis is *not* a state of sleep. It is a state of conscious awareness, often referred to as an altered state of consciousness. Hypnosis is a relaxed state of the mind we enter daily when our brain wave frequencies slow to the range called "alpha"—which we pass through on the way to and from sleep.

Our bodies become physically relaxed when this state of mind is reached, as in meditation, so an observer could perceive us to be asleep; however, the awareness of a person in hypnosis is heightened rather than lessened. Because the conscious mind has relaxed, the subconscious mind becomes accessible, thus giving us expanded possibilities for change. The power is not with the hypnotist; rather, it is within the minds of each of us as we enter hypnosis. I believe a more accurate definition of hypnosis would be *guided meditation.*

This state of relaxation is familiar to you, although not by the name "hypnosis." Every day you experience *four* different mental states. These states of mind can be measured by an EEG (electroencephalograph).

According to Dr. Barbara B. Brown, author of *Stress and the Art of Biofeedback*, experts vary in their opinions on the exact range of *alpha* and *theta* waves. However, since this is meant to be a HOW TO book rather than a scientific or academic treatise, we will only briefly discuss the four basic mental states shown on the following page.

Levels of Daily Consciousness

Brainwave patterns as measured by an E.E.G. machine

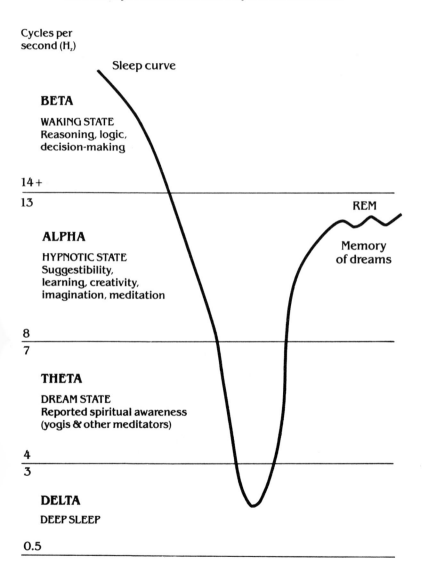

Cycles per
second (H₂)

Sleep curve

BETA

WAKING STATE
Reasoning, logic,
decision-making

14 +

13

REM

ALPHA

HYPNOTIC STATE
Suggestibility,
learning, creativity,
imagination, meditation

Memory
of dreams

8

7

THETA

DREAM STATE
Reported spiritual awareness
(yogis & other meditators)

4

3

DELTA

DEEP SLEEP

0.5

The Four States of Mind

You are in the *beta* state for most of your waking hours. It's a good thing, too, since beta is like high gear, and a good place for decision-making, reasoning, and logic. Brainwaves are above 13 cycles per second, often greatly higher, and may or may not be rhythmic.

As your brain waves slow to between 8 and 13 cycles per second, you enter the *alpha* state of mind. The door between your conscious and subconscious minds is opened, and it becomes easier to access the memory banks of the subconscious— both for recall of memories and storage of new information. We may become mellow in this relaxed state; we are also more creative and imaginative while in alpha. We are also more suggestible— and this is what Hollywood exploits in movies and stage hypnosis. When you are guided into the alpha state of mind by another person or thing, you are technically hypnotized.

Below the two conscious states are *theta*— the dream state— and *delta*— deep sleep or total unconsciousness. Whether or not you remember your dreams, you must pass through theta on the way to and from delta. Likewise, you must pass through alpha on the way to and from sleep. You are in the same state of mind as hypnosis every day of your life!

Hypnosis Is Not Mind Control

Dr. James Braid, the English physician who coined the word "hypnosis," noted that the power is not with the facilitator— but with the person who enters the hypnotic state. Thus, hypnosis does *not* put you under someone's "power." The question I am asked most frequently is, "If this is the case, then why do so many people make spectacles of themselves during stage hypnosis shows?" There are several reasons.

First, a stage hypnotist often prefaces the show by stating that you cannot be made to do anything against your religious or moral beliefs. If you accept that at face value and enter hypnosis, then you have already accepted the unspoken suggestion that you will do anything else!

In reality, you cannot be made to do anything you refuse to do—even in deep hypnosis. My experience with my clients has proven this to me many times. One deepening technique I frequently use is to ask a client to imagine that the left arm feels lighter than air. Yet sometimes, even while definitely in the hypnotic state, clients still reject this suggestion—usually to prove to themselves that choice still exists.

Another reason for the success of stage hypnosis is simply the desire to have a good time. Frequently, the volunteers for a stage show know little about hypnosis, but they expect to have fun. Some may be shy—but given an opportunity to be part of the show and pass the buck to the hypnotist, they become very creative in carrying out suggestions on stage. It becomes comfortable simply to respond and let the hypnotist be responsible. Most volunteers are aware of audience laughter—and are enjoying it themselves. Some, though, merely follow suggestions even if they do not want to because they *think* that they are under the hypnotist's control. They act—or rather, react—according to their beliefs about hypnosis before entering that state.

Often one or two subjects will reject a suggestion even during the show. The stage hypnotist isn't concerned with *why* someone rejects a group suggestion, but a good entertainer will definitely notice those who do not respond and promptly send them back to their seats in the audience.

In the summer of 1984 I attended the show of a well-known stage hypnotist. During the show, a woman indicating signs of a medium depth level of hypnosis rejected two suggestions in a row—and the hypnotist asked her to stand up and return to her table, telling her she was not hypnotized. She accepted that suggestion—and came out of hypnosis while returning to the audience. For those remaining on stage, the unspoken suggestion became very obvious at a subconscious level: If you want to remain in the show, accept the suggestions.

Occasionally someone will do things during the show that they feel comfortable doing only if consciously forgotten—and so they forget. Even if suggested by the hypnotist, this does not automatically happen unless it is desired by the person in hypnosis. However, as I mentioned earlier, many enter hypnosis believing that they are "under the hypnotist's power" during the show. They get what they believe.

I'm not against stage hypnosis. However, I am concerned that for many people stage hypnosis is their *only* exposure to hypnosis. Hypnotherapy and self-hypnosis are useful tools for making the changes we desire in our lives. I would like to see a greater public awareness of the truths and misconceptions about hypnosis—especially since we spend so much of our lives in the alpha state.

How We Enter Alpha

We spend more time in the alpha state than we realize. Earlier I mentioned that we can be guided into hypnosis by a thing as well as by a person. One prime example is television.

Have you noticed how you can be perfectly content watching a good program, then during a commercial break have a sudden urge to raid the refrigerator? You may have drooled over a pizza commercial, but your conscious mind knows that you have a bag of potato chips, so the suggestion given by the sponsor is modified by your conscious mind. The imaginative part of your subconscious produces a brief image of you munching potato chips, and you are on your feet in a flash, headed for the kitchen!

Does this sound familiar? You are responding to hypnotic suggestion when this occurs.

Many parents have noticed a child totally mesmerized by the Saturday morning cartoons. I have had to stand between the television and the child to get acceptance of a simple suggestion such as taking a dirty cereal bowl to the kitchen. The child can be in such a deep state of hypnosis that there is immediate acceptance of the sponsor's suggestion to get the cereal with the toy in the box. The response is so automatic that the little hand is in the grocery bag, opening the box of cereal, even before the groceries have been put away.

In case you think *you* are immune, how often do you remember to ask for cellophane tape, take photocopies, or grab for a facial tissue when you sneeze? And what do you think of if I say, "you deserve a break today, at..."

Another example of our daily trip into the alpha state is at night in bed. I used to get irate at the neighbor's dog barking while I was trying my best to go to sleep. In effect, I would enter the alpha state and think to myself, "I can't sleep with that dog barking!" I had given myself a hypnotic suggestion to be at the dog's mercy!

You can even enter alpha staring out the window and daydreaming— or sitting in church listening to a sermon— or watching a movie in a theater.

Music (even hard rock) can also induce an alpha state. Many of my clients have commented that they sometimes find listening to music helps them think. Remember that *suggestibility* is only *one* characteristic of the alpha state.

What is important now is for you to be aware that you can enter the alpha state at various times during your waking hours— and that while you are there, what you are imagining goes into your subconscious. Since you are suggestible in this state, it behooves you to be careful about what you imagine or daydream.

Being in a state of meditation is neither good nor bad— it is what you are thinking while there that produces either a positive, neutral, or negative result.

Chapter 3

Mind Power Exercise I: Relaxation

Now that you have read about the alpha state, how would you like to experience it?

The exercise in this chapter is designed to give you exposure to one of thousands of methods of entering an alpha state. If you have learned another method from another book—or from a seminar—use what you are comfortable with as long as it works. The method described here is called *progressive relaxation.*

I suggest you read through this chapter once or twice to become familiar with the contents before you begin using the actual technique. The specific words you will use can vary from the typical session suggested here. However, you should follow the basic format.

Now let's begin the session. Find a comfortable place to recline or lie down. If you wear hard contact lenses, remove them. If you chew gum, throw it away. Also, be certain that your clothing is comfortable.

If possible, unplug your phone or turn on your answering machine—and make certain your pets are not in the same room. Some animals seem to sense the mental peace you feel in the alpha state, and they want to be a part of it. This is fine if you have already accepted that—but I can tell you from experience that it is quite a jolt to be totally relaxed with your eyes closed and suddenly feel a cat pounce on your stomach.

Now that you're comfortable, take several deep breaths. Close your eyes if you wish. Imagine that you are letting go of all of your cares and tensions as easily as you let go of the air from your lungs.

Think to yourself words such as this sample session that follows:

> As I now imagine a relaxing sensation entering my toes, my breathing continues to be free and easy—just as when I sleep. The relaxation becomes more and more real with each breath I take, moving up into my feet. It feels **sooooo good to relax** that it becomes easy, comfortable, and automatic for the relaxation to move up into my ankles. The relaxing sensation becomes more and more real with each breath I take. It now moves up into my calves. All my nerves and muscles just let go, responding to my desire to **relax**. The relaxation moves right on through my knees, going up into my thighs—all the nerves and muscles letting go into a deeper and deeper state of relaxation. My hips relax. It feels **so good to relax,** that the feeling continues right on into my stomach muscles and up around my rib cage.
>
> With each breath I go deeper and deeper relaxed. The relaxation moves on into my lower back, going right up into my shoulders—just as though gentle fingers have just given me a wonderful back rub. The soothing feeling of relaxation moves down through my elbows, going right on out through my hands and fingers. With each breath I go **deeper and deeper relaxed.**
>
> The back of my neck relaxes. My scalp relaxes. It feels **so good to relax** that the feeling of soothing comfort moves into my forehead and temples. With each breath I just go **deeper and**

deeper. *My cheeks relax. My jaw muscles relax.*
My entire body now feels completely relaxed.

At this point you may very well be in a light state
of alpha consciousness. If you try this at night before
going to sleep, you may find yourself sound asleep long
before you finish the exercise. Some of my clients have
informed me that they are asleep before getting past
their knees.

If you still feel considerable awareness, however,
you may wish to deepen the relaxation as follows:

*As I now count from ten down to one, I
become **deeper and deeper relaxed with each
number**—just drifting down into soothing
tranquility.*

Number Ten—*deeper and deeper, relaxing
physically.*

Number Nine—*deeper and deeper, relaxing
mentally.*

Number Eight—*deeper and deeper, relaxing
emotionally.*

Number Seven—*deeper and deeper, relaxing
totally.*

Number Six—*every nerve and muscle relaxes
completely.*

Number Five—*each number helps me go **deeper.***

Number Four—*the deeper I go, the easier it is to go
even deeper.*

Number Three—*just drifting into a totally
relaxed state of mind and body.*

Number Two— drifting into a **deeeeeep hypnotic peace.**

Number One—waaaaaay down deep.

You may notice your mind tends to wander. In fact, it may wander considerably as you go deeper into the alpha state. You may have to keep bringing yourself back to each new number, sometimes forgetting the last number you were on. If this happens, just go on with the first number that comes to your mind. Some of you may have to count down twice to go deeper, or count from a higher number. I know some people who start the countdown with 20— and a few who start with 100. You make the choice.

Another technique of the imagination you can use to help you go deeper is to picture yourself going down an elevator.If you don't like elevators, try an escalator, a slide, or steps. You could also be sinking into a cloud, walking into the woods, or lying on a beach listening to waves of relaxation.

There is a possibility you will drift off to sleep during this exercise, so be sure to set an alarm unless it is a convenient time for a nap! If you find that you are aware when you count down— as most people are— then you may come back to full *beta* awareness by simply telling yourself that you feel wonderful and wide awake at the count of *five.* Then count from one to five either mentally or out loud.

The degree of success varies from person to person. Some of you may find this relaxation technique works great the very first time. Others may have to practice, as I did. In fact, I was under so much stress when I first tried self-hypnosis that I had to go to a hypnotherapist for post-hypnotic suggestion to help me make self-hypnosis work.

As you develop your ability to relax in this manner, you may find yourself able to enter an alpha state easily by taking two or three deep breaths and thinking the word *"relax"* each time you exhale.

Practice this exercise before doing the others in this book. If you feel you need help, a cassette tape on *relaxation and stress management* is available (order cassette #103, "Deep Relaxation and Restful Slumber," from the listing in the back of this book), or you can find a hypnotherapist in your area to work with you. (Refer to the questions and answers in Appendix I for tips on finding a qualified hypnotherapist in your area.)

Good luck!

Session One
Review

A. Introduction
1. When your conscious and subconscious are in conflict, your _____ invariably wins.
2. The subconscious tends to resist change.
3. Accept responsibility for yourself.
4. In order to make change permanent, you must change your subconscious "tapes."
5. This book was written to teach you *how* to change your subconscious program tapes.

B. What Is Hypnosis?
1. Hypnosis is a state of conscious awareness.
2. In alpha we become more imaginative, creative, suggestible, and are open subconsciously.
3. We go in and out of alpha regularly, so it is important to be aware of what we imagine.
4. Hypnosis could be called guided _____.
5. All "power" is within the individual, not the hypnotist—therefore, hypnosis is *not* mind control.

C. Progressive Relaxation Method for Self-Hypnosis
A simple method of entering alpha is to progressively relax all parts of your body while in a comfortable position, count backwards to deepen the state, and count forward when you return to normal activity. Or, use the cassette tape #103.

Session Two

**The Power of
Subconscious
Programming**

Chapter 4

Why Program the Subconscious?

What do motivational seminars and New Year's resolutions have in common? They are both generally forgotten by the following week. Why? They frequently contain valuable material, but the desire to change is only at the conscious level. And remember—in a battle between your conscious and subconscious minds, the subconscious invariably wins!

This is because our minds are like computers. A computer terminal accepts input, and the computer always gives the same output until either the input is changed or the program is changed. This is also true for the subconscious mind.

When you try to change a habit pattern or a way of thinking by simply changing the input without changing the subconscious "program," the old habit pattern can be triggered by replaying the original program.

For example, a friend of mine decided to stop smoking and simply did not buy any more cigarettes. Two months later, she subconsciously picked up a friend's lit cigarette while having a cup of coffee. Because she believed she had "blown it," she was back to smoking two packs a day almost immediately.

It's also important to note that it's impossible to have a "blank tape" in your subconscious mind. Either you're in control of your own programming, or you're giving over control to someone else.

Salespeople often have ups and downs because they let others get into their subconscious minds and influence their belief systems. When I was a sales manager, one man on my unit would consistently get all fired up after an inspiring motivational seminar. He would make several sales calls, possibly several sales—then go into a three-week slump when one prospect canceled an order. The top producer in the district said, "So what? I lost one yesterday, but I just went out and got another one!"

The consistent good producer believes in success at a subconscious level. The person held back by subconscious doubts could easily be working twice as hard and getting only half the results. Both people could even have equal talents and ability—yet for one, things just happen! The other person keeps investing a chunk of hard-earned commissions in yet another self-help seminar hoping to find an answer.

The only lasting solution is to *change the subconscious. program.*

Chapter 5

Five Methods of Subconscious Programming

Fortunately, there are several ways to change our subconscious programming. The five methods discussed on the following pages are all familiar ways of effecting a change. Used alone, each method has a chance of success, and some are more effective than others. In conjunction, these five methods are a powerful tool for implementing your conscious desire for change.

Method 1: Repetition

Practice makes perfect.

How often have you heard this one? Everyone knows that you can learn a new habit by practicing. Your piano teacher insisted on scales; your coach insisted on batting practice; your elementary school teacher drilled you on multiplication tables. Your tennis game or golf game improves with practice. New sales representatives "role play" interviews with the sales manager.

Repetition does work, but it takes time. The amount of time can vary from person to person based on other subconscious beliefs about the ability to acquire a new habit.

Repetition can create a new habit pattern or way of thinking, but have you ever tried to *delete* an old habit by the repetition of avoidance? Many people are surprised to find that when they get onto a bicycle for the first time in years, the subconscious still remembers how to stay balanced.

Old habits can be *replaced* but not *erased.*

Why is it so difficult to learn new habit patterns if repetition really works? There are frequently subconscious beliefs at work that contradict the new habit you are attempting to program.

For example, the smoker I mentioned in the last chapter simply tried to delete an old habit by *not* smoking. She did not buy cigarettes—but the subconscious patterns were neither erased nor replaced. Consequently, when a situation occurred that used to trigger her to light up, she immediately grabbed her friend's lit cigarette without even consciously realizing what she had done!

This same principle holds true in business applications as well. The new insurance agent knows that a certain number of phone calls must be made daily or weekly in order to obtain auto insurance expiration dates from prospective clients. The agent makes the calls consistently for several months, greatly irritated by being hung up on and sworn at several times a day. This does not feel good. The repetition of phone calls is outweighed by the emotional expectation of rejection, and another insurance agent leaves the business.

Sometimes you *can* successfully *replace* an old habit with a new one by repetition. However, if repetition alone is not working for you, other resistance may be working against you at a subconscious level—and it may take more than repetition to deal with it.

Method 2: Desire to Identify

Peer Pressure

How many of you parents have heard your child beg you for something merely because "the kids at school have it" ? Whether or not they wanted the $50 jeans before makes no difference now, because of the desire to be like others.

All of us know the power of peer pressure. Children can do the most illogical things because of the desire to identify with or be accepted by peers. "*I dare you!*" is a common phrase children use to get friends to do something dangerous or stupid. Children sometimes desire to be "grown up" and take up the smoking habit.

Among my clients desiring to become non-smokers, the most common reasons given for having started smoking fall into the category of peer pressure. But of course, that was when we were younger, right? Does age do away with this method of subconscious programming?

The best way to answer that question is to simply realize the billions of dollars made by the cosmetics industry and fashion designers. Lest you men think that applies only to women, what about our habit of dressing in a long-sleeved shirt, tie, vest, and coat on a 95-degree day?

On one hand, it is ludicrous for us to be so uncomfortable—yet I personally choose to buy into the peer pressure of wearing a business suit because it is more acceptable to do so, especially when I appear in a public speaking engagement. One of our lawmakers recently appeared in the Legislature on a hot day in a short-sleeved shirt—and was asked to go home and dress properly. It would have been both logical and comfortable for the other lawmakers to have followed his example, but they stuck to custom. Perhaps some-day tens of millions of businessmen will change tradition; but until they do, we will continue to do something both illogical and uncomfortable—yet justify our actions because of subconscious acceptance of tradition.

Mentor

The desire to identify extends beyond peers. A mother might say to her child, "You're just like your father!" Now the child may be prone to copy the father's habits and mannerisms—both good and bad.

A management trainee may look up to a mentor and start using the same "power phrases" and business jargon. The new employee may even dress the same and hold a coffee cup the same way as the mentor, consciously or subconsciously assuming that the path to success lies in imitation.

When you choose to be like someone you admire, you tend to pick up that person's characteristics, habits, and mannerisms; and of course, the easy ones come first! Perhaps you have had the experience of hearing yourself laugh like someone else you know—to your surprise! Or maybe you find yourself using a slang expression that somebody at the office uses frequently. Often, whether or not your conscious mind likes the new behavior, it is already adopted because of subconscious acceptance.

This can be very positive if you choose your mentor wisely—and monitor out any traits you do not wish to adopt. However, *when your subconscious is open, what you do not monitor out may come in!*

Group Identification

Do you know someone who justifies an "Irish temper"? Perhaps an acquaintance looks down on you because you don't belong to the same church or political party.

People tend to identify easily with groups—*my* team, *my* fraternity, *my* country. There is a special feeling that comes with belonging. College students go through an initiation to join a fraternity. People of all ages join churches in order to belong. Other people become involved with causes. The desire to belong is universal.

Organizations often capitalize on the *desire to identify* to effectively further their own causes. Since people enjoy belonging, they easily follow orders in order to remain a member of the group. Again, as with identifying with a mentor, this can either be positive or negative depending on the group goals, methods, and degree of individual involvement.

We were shockingly aware of a religious organization that motivated almost 1,000 people to commit suicide in South America several years ago. Many have wondered how that could have been possible—but for most of the group members, the desire to identify with peers and their leader was a strong subconscious motivator. This was certainly an extreme example of group identification, but other subconscious programming tools had also been used within this organization—in fact, *all* the programming techniques mentioned in this chapter!

The *desire to identify* is neither good nor bad; it's simply one method of getting into the subconscious mind. By increasing your awareness, you can be more careful about monitoring the input when you choose to identify with others.

Put in good programming and you get good results.

Method 3: Authority

Ideas presented by a person held in high esteem or in a position of authority often go straight into the subconscious mind.

This is perhaps easier to see with children than adults, although as with all five programming methods, adults are not immune. Third graders, for example, may believe anything that "Teacher says." If they are told that they are good in math, there is even more motivation to do well. Conversely, the child who is labeled "accident prone" may continue getting frequent bumps and bruises.

During my training in Advanced Hypnotherapy, I watched a videotape about a man who had been told by his fifth grade teacher that he could not spell. His mother reinforced the new belief, and he went through almost forty years of life spelling no better than the average fifth grader. As a child, this man had been "programmed" by two authority figures into thinking he could not spell, and he had held that belief for many years. Gil Boyne, an internationally recognized hypnotherapist, worked with him through age regression to help him express the feelings and memories that had been bottled up inside for all these years. Within a month, he was spelling as well as the average adult.

Perhaps you can think of things your parents or teachers said to you that have stayed with you for years. As adults now, we may feel less vulnerable to subconscious programming by authority figures. Our parents no longer run our lives, nor do our former teachers and college instructors. However, the power of authority can still exert a tremendous impact on us in certain situations.

One example happened to a very dear friend of mine. He had been a chain smoker for over twenty years, had thought about quitting, and had tried, and had failed. He finally just decided to go on enjoying the habit. (Of course, this was before my professional entry into hypnotherapy!)

On February 29, 1976, he lit up at the office during a break and experienced severe difficulty breathing. I personally rushed him to the hospital, where he immediately was taken into surgery with a collapsed lung. During his recovery, his doctor came into the hospital room and said: "If you want to live longer than six months, throw your cigarettes away!"

Because my friend's subconscious was totally open to programming by that doctor for health-related ideas, his subconscious totally accepted this strong suggestion given by medical authority. Today, nine years later, he is a very healthy non-smoker.

Of course, when we give credibility to any outside authority, negative programming can be just as powerful. The subconscious doesn't know right from wrong— it merely accepts what the conscious mind allows to enter— *so be aware of what is going in!*

Method 4: Emotion

Your subconscious is very vulnerable to new programming when you are in an emotional state of mind. Furthermore, as the emotions intensify, the imprints go deeper.

You don't have to be a psychologist to know that severe emotional traumas have contributed significantly to mental illness. People get deeply fearful, sad, depressed, or angry and— carried to an extreme— become totally unable to cope. The result can take months or years of professional help to correct.

Although I neither treat nor diagnose mental illness, I recognize the importance for all of us to be careful what we are imagining when experiencing any kind of emotion— because emotion seems to be the most powerful of the five methods of subconscious programming.

Much has been said and written about the importance of controlling our emotions— but I believe in going one step beyond this concept. *We must monitor our thoughts* when we experience any kind of emotion, whether that emotion is positive or negative.

For example, if you get frustrated at your boss or associate and *fantasize how you would like to respond,* you may someday indeed *find those same words jumping out of your mouth before you can stop them.* When you rehearse certain words or actions *mentally* while experiencing emotion, your subconscious records these impressions. This creates the potential for the imagined words or actions to come out automatically at a time or place you might regret.

This does not mean we should never have feelings, because our ability to feel gives us the ability to love— to enjoy— to appreciate the beauty of a sunset— to feel inspiration from beautiful music— to experience ecstasy with someone dearly loved— to know the contrasts between good times and sad times— in short, to *taste life!*

I simply suggest that you raise your awareness of what happens at a subconscious level when you are emotional, so you can monitor the input. Also, be aware that a positive emotion does not necessarily guarantee a positive result, nor does a negative emotion always produce a negative result.

For example, a new private challenged by his drill sergeant in boot camp may become very angry; and while experiencing intense feelings, decide he is a man and is going to prove it! That kind of emotional impetus could be very useful to his career. However, the use of negative emotion for motivation in the business world can be dangerous. I knew a sales manager for a large corporation who used negative emotion to motivate his representatives, and it backfired as a large percentage of his staff resigned. One of the representatives who left was a woman who had been with the firm for over fifteen years. She was not producing to his satisfaction, so he "motivated" her by challenging her ability to sell. (Shortly after her resignation, he was asked to resign.)

There are also numerous examples of negative results from positive feelings. The divorce courts show many negative results from relationships that were established in the glow of positive feelings. Also, many of the people who followed Jim Jones to their deaths were originally drawn into his organization by feelings of love and acceptance.

As a general rule, however, it is *easier to produce a positive result from a positive emotion*; and there is greater risk of negative programming from feelings of anger, sadness, frustration, fear, and guilt. You also may tend to have a greater degree of control over your imagination with positive feelings—but any emotion felt in the extreme opens you wide to sudden and lasting subconscious imprints.

In this manipulative society we live in, consider how many times you have been manipulated by someone else through love or guilt. This manipulation may be positive or negative, but *you* should determine whether or not to "buy into" the manipulation and accept the responsibility for your decision. Loved ones often know exactly which "buttons" to push! And when you yourself attempt to manipulate someone else through guilt, you take the risk that it may backfire. Many good relationships deteriorate quickly because of this dangerous game of manipulation through guilt—"If you really loved me, you'd..." Yet as parents, we may *positively* manipulate our children by rewarding them for good behavior.

If you wish to be less vulnerable to negative manipulation of your emotions by others, Chapter 7 gives you straightforward methods to help you take more control of your life. Your emotions can serve you or you can serve them. The choice is yours.

Method 5: Alpha State

When your mind is in the alpha state, it is also open for new subconscious programming.

As pointed out earlier, hypnosis is simply being guided into this relaxed state of mind by another person or thing. What you are imagining is what goes into the subconscious. For example, if the hypnotist suggests you are at the North Pole, you can say to yourself that it's not logical—and you won't respond to the suggestion. However, if you indeed imagine being there, your body may actually feel cold—and even produce goose bumps. Or you might be sitting in a movie theater watching a film of someone sweating in blistering hot weather and automatically take off your coat and roll up your sleeves.

The person in deep hypnosis can imagine one hand in a bucket of ice and can actually feel the numbness. Better yet, the person in hypnosis can imagine achieving a goal—and the belief that it is possible takes root in the subconscious. Sometimes *you* can initiate what you imagine. At other times, it is easier to allow someone or something to guide you into creative imagination.

Increasing numbers of people around the country can attest to the benefits of hypnosis in attaining goals—whether for personal or business motivation. Many ex-smokers used hypnosis only as a "last resort" after exhausting other methods to kick the habit. Salespeople have enjoyed significant increases in income after only a few sessions. One of my clients ended the year at 245% of quota just three months after her sessions—and within eighteen months became the branch manager. My wife took off sixty pounds by using hypnosis to help her stay with a program of sound nutrition. A black belt immensely improved his timing in the martial arts.

In Summary

Lots of success methods work; but unless your subconscious mind accepts new attitudes and beliefs, the old habits almost inevitably return. And how do you gain that acceptance?

Repetition alone takes too long.

Desire to identify can have drawbacks. (However, you can certainly supplement any plan by admiring a mentor who has already achieved a goal you are working toward.)

Authority is usually the least effective aid to goal achievement, and your subconscious does not recognize you as authority over yourself.

Emotion, properly channelled, can propel you to success, and I highly recommend combining positive emotion with self-hypnosis for success. However, people prone to emotional "highs" can also be subject to states of depression—negating positive programming. Most sales slumps are self-perpetuating because of the emotional state of mind accompanying the slump.

Hypnosis is the easiest of the five subconscious programming methods to use for attaining your goals. Your ability to consciously plan the proper road and monitor what is taking place subconsciously is greatly increased.

One immediate benefit you can obtain from hypnosis is to gain more control over your emotions—particularly the negative ones. Of course, it is easier to decide to control your emotions while you are feeling calm. This is logical. When feelings of anger, anxiety, or fear suddenly flood the awareness, however, it becomes much more difficult to control these emotions—unless you have practiced! You have the ability to actually practice your emotional responses while in self-hypnosis; and since emotions play an important role in achieving success, emotional control becomes vital.

Chapter 6

The Quintuple Whammy

Now that you've read about the five methods of subconscious programming, let's talk about putting them together.

Obviously, the more impact you have at a subconscious level, the stronger the idea, belief, or "program tape" becomes in your own subconscious.

In the world we live in, we often feel a conflict because there is desire to change as well as desire to resist change. What is happening is that we experience subconscious input to make a change while we yet experience contradictory subconscious input to stay the same.

This is why it is so important to be aware of all five methods of subconscious programming—as it is sometimes necessary to use *all five methods* in order to overcome the strength of the negative input working against you.

I call this the *quintuple whammy.*

To keep this chapter simple, let's use weight control as a sample goal, as it is easy to identify the sources of negative subconscious programming.

Hypnosis Alone is Not Enough

Hypnosis alone cannot make anyone control a habit—it can only make it easier for you to replace a bad habit with a good one, provided you have already decided you wish to make the change. Hypnosis allows you to visualize or daydream your desired change while you are more imaginative, thus making impressions on the subconscious. But *you must still make the appropriate conscious choice.*

Sometimes a client will say, "I'm listening to your tape but I still eat between meals." It's as though they expect me to suddenly make them thirty pounds lighter—but it doesn't work that way. Let's analyze what's happening.

Two methods of subconscious programming are being used to create a new program tape—hypnosis and repetition. There could be a third method—peer pressure to weigh thirty pounds less.

Four methods are working against the person: (1) There is an emotional feeling of comfort that comes with putting something into our mouths. We have been subconsciously "rewarded" and "comforted" with food since childhood; as adults, we need to find other ways to reward ourselves. (2) There is peer pressure to overeat at social occasions and lunches. Friends, especially those who are overweight themselves, may insist you join them for dinner or drinks in order to feel more comfortable in your presence. (3) You are bombarded with images of food and drink while in a state of hypnosis in front of the television. (4) All of the above are happening to you *repeatedly.*

Is it any wonder it is so rare for someone to take weight off and *keep* it off?

Combining the Programming Methods

When I work with a client on a weight control program, I emphasize the importance of using as many of the programming techniques as possible in a *positive way.*

Alpha can be used by listening to the tape regularly—and not simply relying on a half dozen sessions alone to do the job. (Hypnosis is usually deeper in private sessions with a hypnotherapist.)

Emotion can be used by fantasizing how good it feels to be at your ideal weight... enjoying that sense of satisfaction at looking good and feeling good... allowing your feelings to get involved with the benefits of the program.

Desire to identify can be used by admiring others who are doing a good job controlling their weight. They are out there! The *desire to identify* is much more positive than envy. Jealousy, a negative emotion that can only work against you, carries with it the underlying belief that you cannot have what the other person has. Replace envy and jealousy with the idea that it is *good* for someone else to be where you desire to be, because it is also good for you to get there.

Authority is important, because you need a *proven plan that really works.* Some fad diets are dangerous, and there are many groups who would like you to believe they know more about nutrition than they really do. If you choose a proven program for weight control, understand that the system is only as good as you make it. Some of my clients, who are also seeing professional weight control counselors, tell me that hypnosis is essential to help them stay on the diet, and the weight control program is essential for authoritative reinforcement.

Repetition of any and all of the above programming methods reinforces impact at a subconscious level. Use of all five methods is almost essential in weight control because of the strength of past programming as well as the continual subconscious bombardment to activate the old tapes.

If you have five methods working for you and three against you, your chance of success is far greater than if the ratio is three to three. Those of you desiring to reduce might be surprised at the results if you can give yourself a *quintuple whammy.*

For goals other than weight control, the above process can actually be easier because the forces working against you may not be as severe. However, for some people old habits and thought patterns could be even harder to change.

One of my goals is to teach my clients to *be aware of* what is being imagined whenever the subconscious mind is open. Awareness of these five programming methods is the *foundation* for understanding this process. With this understanding, *you* can be in control of changes *you* desire to make in your life.

Later chapters discuss setting goals and establishing priorities. Once you have done these exercises, you may wish to refer back to this chapter and the preceding one so that you may identify sources of negative subconscious input and start monitoring them out. Next, you can look for ways to incorporate as many of the methods of programming as possible to give yourself positive subconscious input— and improving your chances for success!

Chapter 7

Mind Power Exercise II:
Stress Management

The **Mind Power Exercise** in this chapter is designed to give you a simple coping technique you can use when you find yourself in a situation of emotional anxiety.

Many books and seminars are available on stress management. No matter how much you try to eliminate stress from your life, however, there are still times when someone will push the wrong button in your emotional makeup—whether at work or at home. A simple signal to your subconscious mind, given by you at the time of stress, can help you feel a much greater degree of control over your emotions.

Since emotion is such a powerful subconscious programming method, I feel it is essential to learn how to use it for our own benefit.

To maximize the benefit, you must practice through "creative daydreaming" while in a state of self-hypnosis. This helps your subconscious mind accept the desired technique at a time when your emotions are not getting in the way. This is like the rehearsal, which any musician can tell you is *essential* before a good performance.

Whenever you are ready to begin, find a comfortable position as suggested in the first practice session. Read and understand the instructions before proceeding, so that you don't have to refer to them once you begin. If you have not already done so, practice the simple self-hypnosis induction given in Chapter 3 until you become familiar with it.

1. Relax and get comfortable. Remember to remove contacts if you wear hard lenses, and remove gum if you chew it.

2. Read the affirmations on stress management at the end of this book. Read them slowly and deliberately—either silently or out loud.

3. Enter self-hypnosis through the method shown in the first practice session or by listening to cassette tape #103.

4. *Daydream* your ability to take one deep breath of air in any situation and actually feel calm, confident, and composed—totally in control of your feelings.

   Make up a scenario in your mind which would require you to use this technique of control. As you do so, actually take a deep breath and think the word *relax* as you exhale.

   Imagine yourself feeling calm, confident, and in control of your emotions. Imagine the situation through to a desirable conclusion with you remaining calm.

5. When you are ready, come back to the beta state by counting from one to five.

Stress Release Options

You have three healthy options for coping with situations producing anxiety or stress:

1. Express yourself immediately but appropriately. Some situations— such as your child doing something dangerous or a sales objection given during a closing interview— require immediate response. You may find emotion reflected in your voice in the first example, and you may even wait until after you have yelled "no!" before taking your deep breath. In the second example and other situations, you may wish to take a deep breath first, then simply express yourself calmly and confidently.

2. Express yourself later at an appropriate time and place. This option might be in your best interest if an associate at work pushes the wrong button in you while others are present. Some people will accept your opinion much more readily in private over a cup of coffee or tea rather than in front of peers.

3. Release and let go— or, forgive and forget. If you do not choose either of the first options, then practice this one. If you think someone else owes you an apology, then *you* are the one in bondage to that belief. By freeing others from their emotional debts, you actually free yourself. Therefore, the key to forgiving the person upsetting you is to also forgive yourself for buying into it.

Most people use other options for stress control, such as *internalizing*. The results vary from person to person: you can take it out on friends or loved ones, take it out on strangers, take it out on the same person at a later date through blowing something up all out of proportion, or take it out on yourself through sickness or becoming accident-prone. Another common option is an uncontrolled, immediate emotional expression. These options are hazardous to your health and happiness!

In going through your scenarios during self-hypnosis, rehearse the three healthy options outlined above. Your response to the actual stress situation is like the *performance*—which is made much easier by proper rehearsal during self-hypnosis. You are giving yourself post-hypnotic suggestions to allow your subconscious to respond immediately to a given signal, and *you* are the one who decides when to give the signal.

This simple technique alone can increase commissions for many salespeople. The reason is that emotion can be transferred from subconscious to subconscious. If you are in sales and you fear losing a sale after an objection, your prospective customer may subconsciously pick up on that fear even if you use every physical technique in the book to cover it up.

Your fear is that you might lose the sale, but your prospect fears making a decision that would later be regretted—so needs time to "think it over." By maintaining control over your own feelings, your confidence also comes across at a subconscious level. Now your prospective customer may either buy with total confidence, leave the door open to a call-back for valid reason, or confidently refuse to buy. Even this last option is preferable to your being brought back time after time by indecision, which can drain your physical, mental, emotional, and financial resources if you let it.

Understand, too, that your degree of success in coping may vary according to the situation at hand—as well as the frequency of use of your new technique. As a muscle is used, it becomes stronger. If it's not used, it will weaken with time.

After you complete this practice session, take note of your opportunities to practice this new skill. Next time you are driving and someone turns left in front of you, take a deep breath and think the word *relax*. If you feel like calling him a "jerk" first, go ahead— as long as you still take the deep breath afterwards. Another great place to practice this skill is on the job. Suppose you are ready to go home after a hectic day at work, and you suddenly find out you have to stay later because someone else didn't finish a job. Take one deep breath, think *relax*, and do what must be done.

If you would like hypnotic assistance, order the self-hypnosis cassette "Deep Relaxation and Restful Slumber" (#103).

Session Two
Review

A. **Why Program the Subconscious?**
    1. The subconscious, in a way, resembles a
        _____.
    2. To permanently change the output, you must
        change the program, not just the input.

B. **Five Methods of Subconscious Programming**
    1. _____
    2. _____
    3. _____
    4. _____
    5. _____

C. **The Quintuple Whammy**
    1. Existing subconscious input often keeps you
        in an old habit pattern.
    2. If you combine all five methods for getting
        your subconscious to accept your goal, you
        are using a _____ _____ and have a far
        greater chance of success.

D. ***Mind Power Exercise* for Stress Management**
    1. Since emotion is powerful, it is important to
        have a subconscious signal established for
        you to be able to calm yourself when you
        choose.
    2. Put the signal into your subconscious by
        "rehearsing" it while in self-hypnosis.

Session Three

**Realizing
Your Goals**

Chapter 8

Overcoming Habits and Failure Attitudes

Now that you've had a glimpse at how your own subconscious mind can be programmed, take a look inward at any habits or repetitious thought patterns you may wish to change. You may recognize the influence of one or more of the methods of subconscious programming.

For example, most smokers started because of the desire to identify with peers or adults. Poor self-image can usually be traced to emotional experiences where parent, teacher, loved one, or peers caused a feeling of rejection. Confidence can be damaged when we buy into the feelings of sadness and frustration over the failure to attain a goal—whether or not that goal is expressed.

Failure Attracts Failure

Failure often attracts more failure only because the feeling that accompanies it intensifies with self-pity. This negative emotion opens the subconscious doors wide, and the "failures" are remembered and played over and over again. Some people refer to this as "playing old tapes." The more you *think* about failure, the more you are apt to fail again.

The cycle can continue and worsen until the feeling is changed! For a salesperson experiencing a self-perpetuating sales slump, the emotion and the slump may change dramatically with a big sale. Depending on the person and the circumstances, however, it could take days, weeks— or even years— to change the basic attitude from that of failure to that of success.

The Law of Justification

One thing making it difficult to change a subconscious habit or attitude— even when you consciously desire to do so— is that your subconscious belief and acceptance cause *justification*. This justification in turn permits more failure because it is now justifiable.

One interesting example was a client who was seeing me for sports improvement. He was a semi-pro bowler who explained that he always got nervous whenever he left the 10-pin by itself. He rationalized this fear by saying, "I always get nervous and miss that spare." After four sessions, his average went up over fifteen pins— because he stopped justifying and starting focusing on the solution.

When I was a sales manager, I heard a speaker at a motivation seminar give a presentation on how to obtain qualified referred leads. He had a system that had a proven success record. It was well-organized, very professional, and it *worked*. Most of my unit joined me in investing money to hear the presentation as well as purchasing the necessary materials for implementing the system. All of us were enthusiastic about it— but a strange thing happened back at the office. Within a month, there was not even one person in the office using the system the way it was designed.

This bothered me at the time, but there seemed no apparent answer. Those who previously produced well continued to do so, and those who didn't continued in their same habit patterns. Neither the good producers nor the low producers were able to attain subconscious acceptance of the new referral method. The enthusiasm generated at the motivational seminar a month earlier seemed short-lived. The low producers reverted to their same old reasons for sales to be down: It's tax time... summer vacation... New Year's... inflation... recession... illness... car trouble... family problems... poor company leadership... insufficient sales support in the office ... unethical competition... bank denied credit... if only...

"If Only..."

This is such a commonly heard phrase that most of us can think of numerous instances where money or success could have been realized *if only* circumstances had been just a little different than they were.

A salesperson: "That sale was good. I had the signed order and would have had the check at delivery *if only* the competition had called one day later."

A realtor: "*If only* the interest rate had not gone up until after the deal closed escrow, I would have closed my biggest transaction to date!"

An athlete: "*If only* the umpire hadn't made that bad call, we would have won the game."

A frustrated employee: "I could have taken my dream vacation last summer *if only* my boss had given me a raise."

Have you ever found yourself trapped by "if only..." ?

This phrase makes it easy to define a problem — and then proceed to justify it. We can easily defeat ourselves by getting emotionally involved with reasons for failure. It is incredibly easy to get caught saying *if only*, then justify the reason for failure. However, as long as this habit is indulged, success has a way of eluding us.

Does this sound familiar? If so, *delete this phrase* from your vocabulary. You must let go of justification before you can successfully deal with a problem, failure attitude, or bad habit.

Until you let go, *it's impossible* to make the desired change. Of course, experts will tell you to determine precisely what the problem is— but if you desire rapid improvement, you must also *define the solution!*

Chapter 9

Defining the Solution

Have you found yourself among the ranks of those so involved with analyzing reasons for blocking total success that you find the success you seek slips further away? By spending your energy searching for roadblocks in your path to success, your subconscious mind may very well be creating new roadblocks for you to find.

The first vital step toward goal achievement is to become *results oriented*. Determine the results you desire, then determine the best method(s) of attaining those results. Once you do so, begin working toward your goal and don't look back!

How far do you think you would get driving down a busy street with your eyes glued to the rearview mirror 75% of the time? In this obvious example, it's easy to see the importance of keeping your attention on the road in front of you. Unfortunately, the road to Success is not as well mapped.

It's easy to get on a detour or off the road entirely when we are aiming for Success. Our society invests much time, money, and effort into studying reasons for failure. Hindsight may bring insight, but to find Success, we need to invest our time and energy in *where we are going* instead of where we have been!

The next chapter deals specifically with defining the solution by giving you guidelines to help you define your goals.

Chapter 10

Setting Goals

There are plenty of books on the market on the importance of setting goals as a requirement for success—yet few people actually follow the advice of experts and take time to define their goals in writing.

One person told me, "I don't need to write down my goals, because I already know what I want." It's just as easy to justify not putting goals in writing as it is to justify failures.

Some people simply do not want to take the time to list goals in writing. *If a goal is worth working for, it's worth a few minutes of your time to write it down.*

If you don't agree with this, then skip both this chapter and the next. If your goals are already well-defined, then you may go right on to **Mind Power Exercise** III-B.

In a way, taking the time to record a goal on paper is like deciding on a destination for an automobile trip. First you imagine being there, then you decide on a route. Your route may provide scenery or side trips to enjoy along the way. Attainment of a goal may involve several methods to help get you where you are going— with one or more enjoyable (or not-so-enjoyable) activities or detours necessary for arrival at your final destination. Deciding on a method of attainment is like looking at the roadmap to plan your route. Done properly, this helps convince your subconscious mind that the goal is attainable.

I feel it's not necessary for me to further emphasize the importance of putting your goals in writing. The rest of this chapter is simply designed to give you guidelines to make it easier for you to list goals according to types and categories, whether they are personal or business goals.

Goal Types

There are three main types of goals:

Short term

Intermediate

Long term

Short Term

Short-term goals are realistic goals that are attainable within the near future, such as up to a year from now. Examples of short-term goals might be to buy a new car or to work toward a promotion. Some people prefer to think of them as achievable from within one to six months, rather than a year, while others consider a goal to be short term for up to two years from the present. My personal short-term goals are for one year or less, but you should feel free to define your own limits.

Intermediate

Intermediate goals are attainable within one to five years. Examples of intermediate goals might include a trip to Europe or building your own home. Some of you reading this may already be able to take a trip to Europe on a few days' notice, so the goal that is intermediate for one may be a short-term goal for another. As with short-term goals, opinions vary on the definition of "intermediate." Some people prefer to think of intermediate goals as attainable within ten years.

Long Term
Long-term (or life) goals are major life-changing successes for you that may take longer than five years to accomplish. Examples of long-term goals are setting up retirement plans, making long-term investments, or sending all the children through college. In listing goals, many people prefer to mix these with their intermediate goals rather than separate them.

Goal Categories

Now that we have briefly examined the types of goals, let's look at some categories to help you define what is important to you. The main categories are:

Achievements

Possessions

Characteristics

Projects

Changes

More than one type of goal can fall within any category.

Achievements
Achievements are personal or business accomplishments you would like to enjoy. A personal achievement might be to take a trip around the world. A business achievement might be to attain recognition in your field or reach a sales quota (or publish a book!).

Possessions

Owning a new car could be either a short-term or intermediate possession-type goal. Owning your own business could be a short-, intermediate-, or long-term goal.

Characteristics

Things you want to BE could be defined as characteristics. For example, you might want to be the president of an organization— or you might want to be the leading sales representative of the year. You might want to be a mellow person, more confident, or more outgoing, etc. The characteristic can be a position or title, or just a good quality. Of course, certain characteristics could overlap with achievements, as most positions require certain qualifications that could include achievements you must fulfill first.

Projects

These goals could be time-consuming things that you desire to start— or projects that you have already started but would like to finish. Perhaps you started a book last year. Perhaps you have been thinking about writing a book but keep putting it off because it might become too time-consuming. Maybe you started to finish the basement two years ago— and the guest bed still sits in a room with unpainted walls. Perhaps you would like to assist with a church project or get involved in a political campaign.

Changes

Changes involve habits or ways of thinking. Improving your self-image involves a subconscious belief about yourself. Deciding to stop smoking is a change of habit. Once you learn something subconsciously, you cannot "erase" it— but you can *replace* the habit with a positive one. Again, there can be overlap between *changes* and *characteristics*.

Using the above guidelines to trigger ideas, list your goals on a separate sheet of paper. You may wish to use one side for short-term goals and the reverse for intermediate and long-term goals. It's not necessary to determine which category or categories a goal belongs to. The above information is supplied only to make it easier for you to think of goals at a conscious level.

Some people like to separate personal or family goals from career goals, but my personal preference is to mix them. Anything important to me in my career is also important to me personally.

If your first listing of goals produces fifteen or less, then you should combine them all before doing the exercise in the next chapter. If you have a substantial quantity, you may wish to do the exercise once for short-term goals, then a second time for intermediate and long-term goals.

After you've listed the goals you are conscious of, repeat **Mind Power Exercise** I. Immediately after returning from alpha to beta consciousness, look over your list and add anything new that comes to your mind. You might be surprised!

Once you have established your goals, you are ready for the next **Mind Power Exercise**.

Chapter 11

Mind Power Exercise III-A: Establishing Priorities

This exercise is designed to combine logic with feeling to help you determine your priority goals. Please read and review this chapter thoroughly before you begin the exercise to be certain you understand the instructions. To do the exercise properly, you should make a photocopy of the chart on the next page rather than trying to use scratch paper.

When you actually *set* your priorities, you should be in a light alpha state or just returned from one— but make sure you are fully alert while you are reading and comprehending the instructions. The instructions seem simple, but it is much easier to complete the exercise properly if you understand what to do *before* you enter self-hypnosis. Although the instructions are summarized on the chart itself, *read the rest of this chapter* before doing the **Mind Power Exercise**, and refer to the completed sample chart. You must totally understand the instructions while alert in order to follow them while in an alpha state.

Formula for Prioritizing Goals

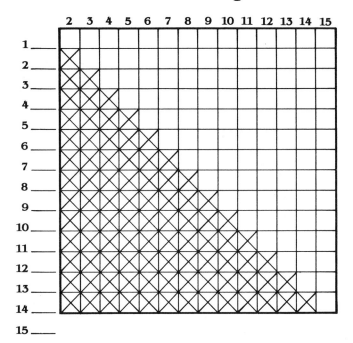

Compare Goal #1 with **each** other goal. Indicate preference by writing the number of the stronger goal in the box below the appropriate number.

EXAMPLE: If Goal #7 is more important than Goal #12, write "7" in the HORIZONTAL ROW 7 under VERTICAL ROW 12. If #12 is more important than #7, you would write "12" in the same spot instead.

Note that many boxes are marked with an "X" to prevent you from comparing the same two goals with each other twice.

SCORING: Count one point for each time you have written a preference for each goal. Notice that scoring is simplified by the fact that numbers can ONLY appear in their respective horizontal or vertical rows.

The goal with the highest score is your PRIORITY GOAL. Other goals can be ranked by preference according to their scores.

Step 1: Number Your Goals

Make a list of *all* your goals. Number your goals in the order you have listed them, without regard to type or category. If you have over fifteen goals, you may wish to segregate them according to short term and intermediate or long term.

If you still have over fifteen short-term goals, you may do one of two things: (1) extend the chart with additional numbers up to the total number of goals you are analyzing, or (2) combine two similar goals ("trip to Europe" and "trip to Orient" could become "take trips abroad").

Step 2: Enter Self-Hypnosis

Get yourself comfortable and have a list of goals, a copy of the chart, and a pen or pencil at hand. Enter self-hypnosis as you have previously practiced, only going in part way. When you feel more relaxed, open your eyes and proceed with the exercise. You should be feeling somewhat mellow, even though consciously aware.

If you are feeling stressed-out, do a long self-hypnosis session before beginning the exercise to give yourself a chance to unwind. If you need to, go through the session on stress management or give yourself some time to listen to your favorite music before attempting this **Mind Power Exercise**.

Step 3: Using the Chart

On the following pages I have listed a sample set of goals and a completed goal chart. Use this example to follow along with the instructions below, until you become comfortable with the method.

Place your page of numbered goals next to your copy of the blank chart.

Notice the column of numbers going down the left side of the chart. When you begin, you are to start with #1 in *that* column and read your goal #1—then compare it with your goal #2. Choose the more important between the two goals (according to the instructions in Step 4), and mark your choice by writing "1" or "2" in the box *below* #2. (My chart indicates that goal #2 was more important than goal #1.) Now compare goal #1 with goal #3 and mark your choice in the box *below* #3. Do this until you have compared goal #1 with each other goal. When you have finished comparing goal #1 with each other goal, you should have *only the top line* of the chart completed.

Now go on to goal #2 and do the same thing again. Notice that there is one less box. Since #2 and #1 have already been compared, there is no need to have another box for comparing #2 with # 1. (To make the chart easier to use, I have X'd out any squares that will never be filled in.)

Sample Goal List

1. Buy new home
2. Publish book
3. Pay off all debts
4. Enjoy abundant cash flow
5. Own a new Mercedes free and clear
6. Establish average work week under 50 hours
7. Take trip to Greece
8. Take trip to Australia
9. Get new office furniture
10. Establish more branch offices

Formula for Prioritizing Goals

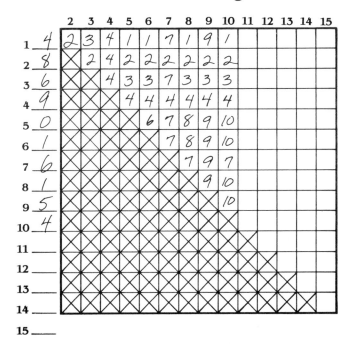

Compare Goal #1 with **each** other goal. Indicate preference by writing the number of the stronger goal in the box below the appropriate number.

EXAMPLE: If Goal #7 is more important than Goal #12, write "7" in the HORIZONTAL ROW 7 **under** VERTICAL ROW 12. If #12 is more important than #7, you would write "12" in the same spot instead.

Note that many boxes are marked with an "X" to prevent you from comparing the same two goals with each other twice.

SCORING: Count one point for each time you have written a preference for each goal. Notice that scoring is simplified by the fact that numbers can ONLY appear in their respective horizontal or vertical rows.

The goal with the highest score is your PRIORITY GOAL. Other goals can be ranked by preference according to their scores.

When you have completed this part of the exercise, each goal should have been compared *once* with each other goal you have listed—and your choice indicated in the appropriate box.

Step 4: Making the Choice

You may use one of two methods for making your selections, according to your personal preference.

The first method involves asking yourself, "If I could have *only one* of these two goals, which one would I desire the most?" This gets into your "gut feelings" to help you determine how important some goals are. This is the method I personally use most of the time when I do the exercise.

The second method involves asking yourself, "Which of these two goals do I desire *first?*" This is a more intellectual approach, useful for deciding what you should work on chronologically; however, it does not lend itself for use with goals of mixed types. Use this method only if you have segregated your short-term goals from your intermediate and long-term goals.

Once you choose which method to use, *be consistent!* The only exception: if you are totally undecided between two goals, break the tie by using the alternate method—but remember to return to your original method for your next choice.

Step 5: Scoring

Once you finish comparing all the goals, come up to total conscious awareness by counting from one to five. Stand up and stretch to be sure you are fully alert.

Now, count the number of times the number "1" appeared in any box. Write that number in the column to the left of the chart (in my example, #1 appeared four times). Now count all your #2's and do the same. Continue until you have counted all the occurrences of each number. If you have done the exercise properly, *the number of each goal selected* should appear only *below* or *to the right of* the same number printed on the chart.

Note the goal that was chosen the most times. This is your new #1 goal.

Step 6: Assigning Priorities

Renumber your goals according to priority by listing those with the highest scores first. New goal #1 becomes the goal with the highest score— then continue down to the one with the lowest score, your least important goal. It may become necessary to break ties as explained below.

Break a two-way tie by determining which of the two goals you chose during the exercise. For example, note on the sample that goals #3 and #7 each scored 6 points. Since #7 was chosen when these goals were compared against each other, #7 ranks higher in importance than #3— even though they both scored the same.

Break a three-way tie by selecting the most important or eliminating the least important of the three, then using the method above to determine the order of the other two.

Step 7: Evaluating the Results

Review your goals in the order of priority. (My sample goal list in its new order of priority is shown on the next page.) You may wish to rewrite your reordered goals on a fresh sheet of paper so your priorities will stand out clearly.

You may have one or two surprises!

Frequently a goal you think is important comes out low on the list, and a seemingly unimportant one comes out high. This does not disprove the validity of the exercise; rather, it points out why you should periodically do this exercise. I personally prioritize my own goals in this manner about once every three months.

As time passes, you may find yourself adding new goals and, hopefully, deleting old ones that you have reached.

Sample Goal List
With New Priorities

1. Enjoy abundant cash flow
2. Publish book
3. Take trip to Greece
4. Pay off all debts
5. Get new office furniture
6. Buy new home
7. Establish more branch offices
8. Take trip to Australia
9. Establish average work week under 50 hours
10. Own a new Mercedes free and clear

In Conclusion

Remember that the results are more accurate if you do the comparisons according to your feelings rather than by logic. By being in a light alpha state while comparing your goals, you are more in touch with your true feelings. Now you can have more confidence that the goals at the top of your list are the ones that really matter to you.

Knowing which goals are important is almost as important as having those goals defined in the first place. If you are putting energy into a defined goal that has little importance to your own happiness—just because your intellect, boss, or a loved one tells you it should be important—then you could experience a certain amount of frustration. You can still choose to work toward that less important goal, but by putting equal or greater energy into your own *priority goals*, you are more apt to be happy as well as successful.

Remember that happiness is a state of mind—and it is possible to experience intellectual or financial success and be miserably unhappy in what you are doing because it is not what you really desire the most. Reaching the goals that are important to *you* can be immensely satisfying.

Also remember that you have a right to change your mind. Feelings can change with circumstances. If you repeat this session six months from now, you may notice differences in the order of your goals. However, since your own feelings *are* involved, it is important for you to be in a peaceful state of mind while prioritizing.

Once you *consciously* know which goals are more important to you at an emotional level, go on to the next chapter.

Chapter 12

Planning Your Course

Now that you know which goals to work toward, you must plan your course.

This book does not suggest *which* success method you should choose. Much has already been written on the importance of proper planning: sales techniques that work for both prospecting and closing, effective weight control programs, methods of minimizing stress, proper ways to hold a tennis racquet or a golf club.

At this point, however, you should use any valid source available to help you determine the best method(s) for *you*. A high sales quota is not achieved by simply sitting in the office in an alpha state all day waiting for the telephone to ring—you have to *do something*. Similarly, excellence in music does not come by wishful thinking alone. It comes through practice as well as proper training. And reducing thirty pounds does not come *only* by daily daydreaming in an alpha state. You must also consciously choose the eating and/or exercise habits you desire to program into your subconscious.

If you set off on an automobile trip to Canada, would you just get in your car and head north? Unless you are familiar with the roads, you would have to refer to a road map in order to plan the route that best suited you. The same holds true for goal achievement.

While you are in the alert beta state, you should logically determine what is necessary for you to attain your desired result.

People often come to my office wanting me to "wave a magic hypnotic wand" and suddenly make them thirty pounds lighter without any effort or planning on their part. Hypnosis is not magic, nor does it replace the use of a proven method for obtaining successful results—it only *supplements* a proven method. The main benefit of hypnosis is its use in helping the subconscious mind accept what the conscious has decided to do. *Without that acceptance*, you are defeated before you ever begin!

I encourage you to accept responsibility for making decisions that *you* believe will give you the highest probability of success. First, choose a method you believe can work for you, then use **Mind Power Exercise** to solicit acceptance at the subconscious level.

Now What?

Once you have both the goal and method(s) planned, get your imagination involved with the *benefits* of achieving your goal.

Your subconscious is much more comfortable (and happier) imagining trying on your ideal size of clothes than giving up dessert. In a sense, your conscious mind must *sell* to your own subconscious. Professional salespeople are always told to emphasize *benefits* rather than price. You must also emphasize the benefits to yourself. Your subconscious resists "high pressure sales"—but it can be *persuaded* to change.

An excellent starting point is to combine positive emotion with hypnosis—marrying the two most powerful methods of subconscious programming—to get your subconscious to "buy" the benefits. **Mind Power Exercise** III-B in the next chapter will get you started.

Chapter 13

Mind Power Exercise III-B: Creative Daydreaming

Now let yourself have fun!

As mentioned earlier in this book, alpha opens the door to the subconscious and allows you to be more creative and imaginative.

Emotion also opens the door to the subconscious. Emotion can make you its servant if uncontrolled, or can become your servant when you are in control. Perhaps you have noticed how someone emotionally excited about reaching a goal seems to get there faster.

I'm not talking about using false "emotional hype" in this session; rather, we will use positive controlled emotion added to constructive visualization. You can now combine two of the five methods of subconscious programming with more than double the impact.

Get relaxed and enter self-hypnosis according to the exercise in **Mind Power Exercise** I.

Once you feel you are into the alpha state, imagine that you have already reached your goal. Imagine yourself seeing, feeling, and experiencing it in your mind. *Daydream that it is present reality* ! Get all five of your senses involved. *Feel* that sense of emotional satisfaction as you allow yourself to enjoy the fantasy. Know that as you fantasize your success, you absolutely have the ability to do what it takes to realize this goal. Feel a sense of appreciation to God or to the Universe for making this possible. You are now building faith on a subconscious level—where it gets results.

If you desire a new car, imagine yourself in the driver's seat. Hear the purr of the engine. Smell the new upholstery. See yourself putting the pink slip in a safe place— indicating to your subconscious mind that *you own it yourself.*

If you desire more confidence in closing sales, imagine yourself at your best in a sales interview. Feel your satisfaction when your customer signs the order. See your new client smiling, shaking your hand, and thanking *you* for making your product or service available.

If you desire a sharper golf game, imagine properly addressing the ball. See the club connect. Feel the follow-through. Picture the ball landing on the green, exactly where you want it.

If you desire more money, imagine yourself hold - ing a wad of crisp, new $100 bills. What would you do? How would you feel? Let your imagination run free.

If you desire to take off thirty pounds, imagine standing in front of a mirror looking at a reflection of yourself at your desired weight. Picture yourself wearing the sizes and styles of clothing you desire at your ideal body weight. Feel that sense of satisfaction as you imagine doing things you enjoy at this ideal weight. Imagine you have already been at this weight for a year. Continue with this fantasy in your mind until you actually begin to feel a little excitement about the possibility of *being there.*

During my wife's sixty pound weight reduction, her imagination frequently took her on a shopping spree to her favorite store. She would mentally try on all the size 10's on the rack, then admire herself in the mirror. Her size 10 shopping spree eventually became a reality, and she assures me that the reality is even better than the fantasy!

If you desire a luxury vacation such as a cruise to the Bahamas, imagine yourself sipping champagne on the deck of a ship while you smell the salty sea air.

If you desire to write a book and see it published, picture it already in print— as I have done with this book.

Remember that every invention and innovation originates in someone's mind. When you are in the alpha state, you are more creative as well as imaginative, so you are open to new ideas to flow into your conscious awareness that may contribute to your success. Because of this, you may find yourself discov - ering new methods of goal achievement you never thought of before. The benefits of creative daydreaming can even surpass that of simply programming your subconscious mind to reach the goal in the first place. The new ideas generated by this reprogrammed subconscious can make it even *easier* for you to succeed.

Now it's your turn.

Sit back, relax, and enjoy your daydreams— and may all your dreams come true!

Session III
Review

A. **Overcoming Habits and Failure Attitudes**
    1. Failure attracts _____ because you think about it.
    2. Whatever the subconscious believes is justified.
    3. Remove "if only..." from your vocabulary.

B. **Defining the Solution**
    1. Become results oriented.
    2. Know what you want and *go for it.*

C. **Setting Goals**
    1. If a goal is worth working for, it is worth
        _____ .
    2. Use the guidelines in Chapter 10 to help you define your goals.

D. **Establish Priorities Using** *Mind Power Exercise* **III-A**
    This exercise combines alpha with logic. Read the instructions carefully before doing the **Mind Power Exercise.**

E. **Plan Your Course**
    1. Your use of the subconscious programming tools can help you achieve goals—but *you* must choose those goals as well as your course of success.
    2. Sell your goal to your subconscious.

F. **Use Creative Daydreaming to Get the Feel of Your Goal**

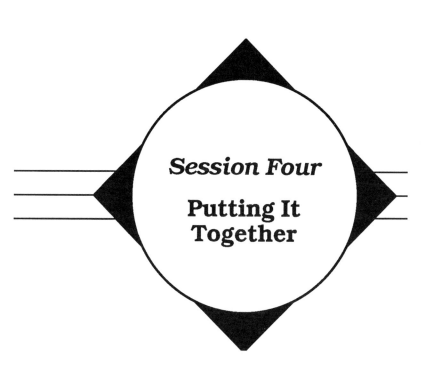

Session Four

Putting It Together

Chapter 14

Designing Effective Affirmations

Affirmations— positive statements of belief— are popular in the 80's, but few people seem to know how to properly structure and use them.

Used wisely, affirmations can be powerful tools to help you create success attitudes in your subconscious mind. If misconstructed or misused, however, they can actually move your goal further from reach.

One highly respected organization suggested to its salespeople that they write this affirmation and tape it to the dash of their automobiles: "*I don't quit until it hurts!*" The intent behind this was to motivate each representative to make that one last call. In reality, however, use of the above "affirmation"— if you can call it that— would give the subconscious *two negative messages*. First: *prospecting hurts.* Second: *when it does, you can quit!*

When I sold insurance, I was told that everyone has "call reluctance," because it comes with the territory. How many salespeople have accepted this fallacy as their reality? In management school we were taught that nobody likes to make prospecting calls, but it was necessary to motivate our representatives to do so anyway in order to secure an adequate number of appointments. A commonly used affirmation was "*thirty calls daily equals ten interviews weekly equals three sales per week.*" This formula kept me in the business for years, but did not address the issue of telephone confidence. After my first three years in the business, I still hated the telephone just as much as ever. In fact, I used to spend seven hours in the rain doing "cold prospecting" (and it really *was* cold out there!) to businesses in order to avoid one hour's telemarketing. (I later discovered that you don't have to hate the telephone.)

We are also told to expect objections. I have given many sales presentations where I totally expected a new client to proceed with the recommendations because I knew they were sincere and logical— only to find the person signing willingly before I even had a chance to "close" the sale with a formal closing question. There were also times I felt doubts about the sale— and sure enough, I got exactly what I expected: *no sale*!

What Is Expected Tends to be Realized: The Principle of the "Self-Fulfilling Prophecy"

One basic natural law is that you tend to get whatever you believe at a subconscious level. The purpose of an affirmation is to help convince your subconscious mind of the possibility of what you already consciously know.

Affirmations can help you do that only if they are both properly structured and properly used; otherwise, they can actually become counterproductive. When my first marriage broke up, my sales hit rock-bottom even though I had previously been among the leaders. I heard someone I respected highly say, "Nobody does well in sales for two years after a divorce!" Because I was in an emotional state, this negative idea went into my subconscious like an affirmation. I found myself going through all the mechanics of sales success as in previous years, but without satisfactory results. I read self-help books and used affirmations continually, wondering why they would not work. Today I know what happened.

Wording Is Vitally Important

One of the self-help books I read during this period gave numerous examples of affirmations about avoiding fear and eliminating poverty. The basic concepts and ideas— as well as most of the sample affirmations—were valid. However, the wording was *incorrect* on some that I personally chose to use, so the more I used them the less they seemed to work.

As a hypnotherapist, I now understand the importance of semantics when dealing with the subconscious. Affirmations are like hypnotic suggestions and must be constructed similarly— except that they are stated in the first person.

Use the guidelines below to prepare several affirmations about your #1 priority goal.

Use Positive Statements

Positive statements to our subconscious minds are much more effective than negative ones. For example, if you say, "I am not afraid," your subconscious mind ignores the negative— and you are still claiming the fear. A better way of stating this is:

I am confident.

I have seen many "affirmations" recommended for personal or professional improvement that focus on the *problem* to be avoided rather than on the *solution*. (Specific examples are included in the next chapter.)

To illustrate, try sitting back, relaxing, and having a friend read the following paragraph to you:

Take a deep breath. Close your eyes and relax. Picture a grassy meadow in Africa with a few bushes and trees nearby. Now— *do not think of an elephant!*

Was it gray or pink?
This is called *the law of reversed effect.*
Most people will immediately think of an elephant— yet the person wanting to stop smoking gets emotional while thinking, "I can't have a cigarette— I don't want one." The result is a nagging feeling of deprivation, because the subconscious mind does not like to be told NO— and the craving simply increases. Since you cannot simply delete the wrong image by telling yourself NO, you must *replace* that image with a new, *positive* one.

In a very rare circumstance you may find it necessary to state a problem in order to affirm the solution in the same statement. Should you feel this essential, put the problem in the *past tense* and the method of coping in the present. For example:

Whenever something occurs that used to cause stress, I take one deep breath and remain calm— totally in control of my feelings.

Affirm the Solution

Another law of the mind is called the *law of awareness.* In simple terms, it means that you tend to attract whatever you remain most aware of. As you put mental energy into the problem, you tend to magnify its effect at a subconscious level. It becomes imperative, then, to use affirmations that focus the subconscious on the result— or method of attaining the result— rather than on avoidance of the problem.

Examine the statement, "*I am in control of my temper.*" It sounds harmless enough, but nonetheless the user of the above "affirmation" is claiming ownership of a temper rather than a calm disposition. A better way of stating this would be:

I am a calm person.

Use the Present Tense

If you give your subconscious an escape hatch, it will use it.

By making the statement, "*I will control my eating habits,*" you give your subconscious permission to wait until tomorrow— and we all know that tomorrow never comes! Furthermore, on the slight chance that tomorrow might just possibly arrive someday, your subconscious may trick you into eating even greater amounts of "junk food" while it is still today! The statement should be rephrased:

I am in control of my eating habits.

Sometimes your own emotion prevents a statement from being believable in the present tense. For example, my wife found it impossible in the early months of her weight reduction to use the affirmation, "*I am slender and sexy .*" One simple change, however, made the affirmation totally acceptable at a subconscious level:

Each day I am becoming slender and sexy.

Even though the conscious mind knows this is yet future, present improvement is implied— and this is very comfortable to the subconscious mind.

Be Specific

The subconscious knows no jokes, so you must carefully state exactly what you desire—without using slang expressions or words that have double meanings.

Let's look at a seemingly acceptable affirmation: *"My good eating habits help me lose excess weight."*

Can you see the subtle escape hatch for the subconscious in the above statement? We have been subconsciously programmed since childhood to find what we lose! Yet how many people do you know who are trying to "lose" weight? You can reduce, discard, release, throw away, give away, take off, get rid of, eliminate, or toss out excess pounds—but don't tell your subconscious that you "lost" weight last month unless you are below your normal, healthy weight and wish to find what you lost.

Here's another example: "I want money." Want implies lack—and even if you get money, it may be from cash advances on credit cards or from selling possessions out of necessity, unless you are more specific. A better affirmation would be:

I create more income in ways that are good for all concerned.

Saying that you create *more* income tells your subconscious that you already have some. Another way of stating a similar affirmation might be:

I appreciate my increasing supply of money.

"I am—"

There is power in those two words. Use them often in your affirmations to describe how you are, how you act, and how you feel about the reality of your goal. For example:

I am thankful for my increasing success.
I am more confident with each passing day.
I am enjoying the right uses of money.

Write Your Affirmations

Using the above guidelines, write your own personal affirmations for successfully attaining your priority goal. Remember to be specific, keeping all your statements in the present tense. ("I am happier now," rather than "I will be happy.") You may affirm method as well as end result. You may also affirm the proper attitudes and your own personal belief in the successful attainment of your goal. It is very important that you do this *before* attempting **Mind Power Exercise** IV.

The next chapter shows examples of improperly written affirmations— all of which have been recommended by others. The better way of making each statement follows, along with the reason(s) for the changes.

Chapter 15

Editing Your Affirmations

Review your personal affirmations slowly and carefully while you are in a relaxed state of mind. Add any new ones flowing through your thoughts at the time. Delete or change any existing ones that are not totally comfortable to you.

As you go through each statement, allow yourself a little emotional feeling of satisfaction as you progress toward your goal. Your logical mind may rationalize that you are not making progress at the time because you are not physically doing anything to earn money, take off weight, etc. You must bypass these "logical" arguments and realize that this is time well spent! By programming your subconscious mind properly, you can work smarter rather than harder. To ensure success, it's vitally important that you edit your affirmations.

After you have examined your affirmations in a meditative state and made whatever changes are appropriate, go back once again to a beta state to make certain they are all properly worded according to the guidelines mentioned in the previous chapter. Read through the next section on "Examples of Editing Affirmations" and then immediately read your own.

Again, be certain you are in *beta* with your logical mind aware as you do the final edit of your own affirmations. I have seen printed examples of affirmations where over half of them contain "self-destruct" words or phrases. I have also found and eliminated self-destruct wording in my own affirmations even *after* my first edit.

Examples of Editing Affirmations

Now let's look at some affirmations that have been recommended by others and examine the reasons for improving their structure:

1. *I will be more confident with each passing day.*

   The word "will" is in the future tense, so the subconscious mind has a reason for non-compliance since tomorrow never comes. A better way of stating it would be:

   I am expressing more confidence each day.

2. *I am willing to release the situation causing my present condition.*

   "I am willing to" does not say that the releasing is actually being done. The above statement also justifies the present condition because of the existence of a "situation." A better way of phrasing would be:

   I now release the past, and am improving the present.

3. *I don't get angry without just cause.*

   If you use the above statement, your subconscious could claim the anger and then proceed to find cause to justify the emotion. It is far better to state the desired solution:

I am calm and in control of my feelings.

4. *I easily forgive people who do me wrong, under standing their weakness.*

    Again, the above statement claims reality to a problem. Using it could invite your subconscious to cause you to look down on others because they are "weak" and don't measure up to your standards. A much more positive statement is:

    I am a forgiving and understanding person.

5. *By avoiding bad foods I am losing my excess weight.*

    The subconscious does not like to be deprived, so it's better to talk about eating good foods. Also, "finders keepers, losers weepers!" is a phrase we learned as children, so let's discard or release the excess weight:

    My good eating habits help me release excess weight.

6. *Whenever I get stressed out I simply take a deep breath and RELAX.*

    If you desire to state what to do when a problem does occur, put the problem in the past tense with the solution in the present tense:

    When something happens that used to get me stressed, I simply take a deep breath and relax, remaining calm.

7. *I am prosperous.*

This is a very positive statement if you already believe you are prosperous. If you do not believe it subconsciously, then some slight modification may increase the possibility of subconscious acceptance:

I am continually becoming more prosperous.

8.   *I always have enough money to pay my bills.*

How about having some left over for yourself? Rather than simply affirming just enough money to "get by," try the following:

My income continues to exceed my expenses.

9.   *I see failure as the the negative feedback I need to change my course.*

This statement claims failure, admits you have *needs*, and affirms that you are headed in the wrong direction. Let's make it positive:

What others perceive as failure, I perceive as a learning experience helping me to improve my present course.

10.   *I love objections, and each NO gets me closer to the sale.*

If you love objections, you'll get them—and still think of them as objections to buying rather than concerns of ownership. The second part is tricky, because no salesperson bats a thousand; however, we can still edit as follows:

I give wise and appropriate responses to customer (or client) concerns because they indicate interest, moving us closer to the best decision. I accept that each interview has value regardless of the final decision.

11.   *I realize we are NOT our body, actions or Aware ness and that blame and guilt are NEVER valid because any fault in what we do lies NOT in us but in our faulty Awareness.*

This one was lifted verbatim from a recent self-help publication. Use your new skills to decide what to do with it:

_____
_____
_____

These are only a few examples. You must understand that your subconscious mind takes things much more literally than your conscious mind, which often overlooks the subtle wording that can sometimes frustrate the objective of an affirmation. Be certain to edit your own affirmations carefully while in a totally alert *beta* state of mind— rewrite them, then edit them a second time for final approval.

Numerous examples of affirmations are at the back of this book in Appendix II. You may feel free to use whichever ones you wish, making changes as you desire. Also feel free to reproduce those pages with the printed affirmations for your own personal use.

Remember that the purpose of affirmations is to help convince your subconscious to believe in your ability to reach your goals. They will also help you become self-motivated, since motivation and subconscious beliefs are so closely related.

Add Your Key Word

Now that your affirmations are ready, you are about to go one step beyond any other self-help book.

zI have read and heard too many times to count that you should read or say your affirmations many times daily. Some who do this manage to put those affirmative statements into the subconscious mind through the *repetition* method of programming—but remember, there are easier ways to get into your subconscious!

Alpha is much faster and easier, and *emotion* is powerful.

Combine these two methods of programming and see how much faster you can make affirmations work for you.

Rather than trying to pick one or two affirmations to say 100 times daily (as one self-help book advocated), you can simply have *one word* which represents an entire group of affirmations to your subconscious mind. You will, therefore, only have to spend time with your affirmations at the time you do your self-hypnosis— or **Mind Power Exercise**.

Your last affirmation should be as follows:

My key word is _____ . Whenever I say, hear, see, or think the word _____ , it automatically reinforces all of these affirma - tions.

Chapter 16

Choosing a Key Word

Many thousands of people all across the country are into what is commonly called "treasure mapping" their success.

Typically, a picture that symbolizes the desired goal is posted somewhere handy (like the refrigerator door). This could be a picture of a Hawaiian beach, a new Cadillac, a handful of money, etc. The benefit of doing this is that the picture is a subconscious reminder to do what it takes to reach the goal.

Key words work much the same way— only in some cases, even better.

We all carry a set of keys to unlock doors. I have a set of key words which unlock certain doors of my own subconscious mind. For example, the word "RELAX" means that I am calm, confident, and in control of my feelings. The word "MONEY" reminds me that money is a tool helping me to express greater love, inspiring motivation for successful business activity. That same word also symbolizes to me an entire page of affirmations on abundance, success, and the right attitudes of acceptance for more money flowing through my life.

You can select a key word for your priority goal, eliminating the need to repeat numerous affirmations dozens of times daily. Once you choose the word, put it into your subconscious by making the last affirmation on your list as follows:

My key word is ____. Whenever I say, hear, see, or think the word _____, it automatically reinforces all of these affirmations.

The benefit of establishing and using a key word to help you succeed can be stated in one sentence: Your KEY WORD helps you put everything together and make it work.

Choosing the Best Word

It's a good idea to choose a word that you are comfortable with both intellectually and emotionally. The word should feel good, but also—directly or indirectly—indicate either your goal or an attitude or method helping you to achieve the stated goal.

Typical key words chosen by clients for success or sales motivation are:

Confident

Confidence

Success

Prosperity

Money

Abundance

Typical key words chosen by clients for weight control are:

Slender

Slim

Trim and fit

Attractive

Shape

Satisfy

Sexy

One weight control client chose the word "self-discipline" at a conscious level—but when I attempted to confirm acceptance of this word in hypnosis, it was quickly rejected. The subconscious was not comfortable with the idea of "discipline" and the word was replaced.

When you have a word in mind for your goal, sit back, relax, and take a deep breath. Close your eyes and ask yourself, "Am I comfortable with this word as my key word?" You should have a feeling of yes or no.

Once you are satisfied with your word, write it down.

How to Use Your Key Word

As previously mentioned, your last affirmation should define your key word. It is also appropriate if several other affirmations contain the same word.

The next **Mind Power Exercise** shows you how to incorporate your key word into your subconscious. It is *up to you* to make certain you use it during the day.

I suggest you put a 3x5 card on your refrigerator door, bathroom mirror, or car dash—anywhere that you will inevitably see it several times daily. If you have chosen a common word, you may find yourself using and hearing the word many times daily in conversation. You can also make a point to think of your word several times daily, at least until you are well on the road to achieving your goal.

As you find yourself reaching a goal, you can still use the same word for another goal requiring the same basic attitude or activities. You can also use other key words for other goals—but don't spread yourself too thin by trying to work on too many goals at the same time.

If you require assistance, contact the American Council of Hypnotist Examiners for the name and phone number of a Certified Hypnotherapist in your area. Write to:

American Council of Hypnotist Examiners
1147 E. Broadway, Suite 340
Glendale, CA 91205
Telephone: 818-247-9379

Chapter 17

Mind Power Exercise IV: Making It Work

Now it's time to combine affirmations, self-hypnosis, creative daydreaming, positive emotion, and key words in order to *make it work*.

Recap

In *Session One* you read about the states of the mind—and what happens when you enter the *alpha* state. Practicing the simple relaxation technique described in that session should have given you at least some exposure to self-induced hypnosis, even if you attained only a light state. By becoming familiar with the feeling, you can become more aware of other times during the day when you might be entering a light *alpha* state of mind at times when you would never have suspected—such as simply staring out the window and daydreaming!

Session Two covered subconscious programming —why it's necessary and how it's done. As explained, hypnosis is only one of five methods; and the more methods you use to change your own subconscious belief patterns about yourself, the greater your probability of success. Emotion is the most powerful of the programming methods, so it behooves you to be the one in control of your emotions. Control, however, does not mean squelching or "internalizing"— so **Mind Power Exercise** II is important. In learning how to handle your own feelings and cope with a stressful situation, you immediately gain a greater level of control over your life. Whether or not you feel on top of the circumstances surrounding your life, you can at least *choose your response* to those circumstances. Practice the stress management **Mind Power Exercise** often until you feel you have a better handle on things. This can benefit you in both your business and personal life!

Session Three discussed changing habits and attitudes as well as setting goals for yourself. Often it's necessary to change an attitude in conjunction with working toward a goal. For example, fear of the telephone can stop a potentially successful sales representative from reaching sales goals. You were asked to list your goals, and shown how to *create priorities* combining logic with feelings. Of course, you must establish a plan of success just as you would plan your route of travel for an automobile trip. You were then asked to have some fun by doing another **Mind Power Exercise** and *daydreaming* that you have already reached your goal! The importance of this is that you can greatly increase the impact on the subconscious by combining hypnosis and emotion; so it's important for you to actually fantasize your sense of emotional satisfaction at achieving your goal when doing creative daydreaming.

So far in *Session Four* we have discussed affirmations, and why it's important to structure them properly. Unless you have decided to read this book through once before doing any of the mental exercises, you should already have a key word chosen for your priority goal. If not, then go back and review the chapter on key words and make at least a tentative selection before doing **Mind Power Exercise** IV.

Now let's put everything together.

Doing It!

As with each **Mind Power Exercise** in this book, you should read the instructions through more than once—enough to become familiar with what to do when you put the book down.

Follow the steps outlined below:

1. Get comfortable as in **Mind Power Exercise** I with your affirmations in hand.

2. Read your affirmations *slowly*. Even if your mind tends to want to wander or skip ahead, you should still keep reading them one word at a time. Reading aloud helps slow you down. It's important to *read each word.*

3. Read the affirmation designating your *key word* at least twice to subconsciously reinforce the association that your key word represents all the affirmations.

4. Remove glasses, contacts, etc., and enter the state of self-hypnosis as in **Mind Power Exercise** I.

5. Once you feel yourself becoming more relaxed and/or imaginative, think of your *key word.* You may say it several times in your mind, or even say it out loud if desired. It's not necessary to open your eyes and review the affirmations, because your *key word* now represents all of the affirmations at a subconscious level. This is the next best thing to actually hearing someone else give you the affirmations as hypnotic suggestions.

6. Daydream that you have already achieved your goal. Imagine doing things you enjoy doing with

this goal a present reality. BE THERE within your imagination! Fantasize your appreciation of the reality of your goal, and allow yourself to be open for any new ideas flowing into your conscious awareness from the creative part of your mind to help you succeed. Remember that the *alpha* state helps you become more creative as well as imaginative—but keep it positive. If any negative thought creeps in, *replace* it. You cannot simply delete it by "trying not to think of it." When a positive idea presents itself, imagine incorporating it into your method(s) of goal achievement. Keep a note pad handy to write down any good ideas immediately upon conclusion of the **Mind Power Exercise** to be certain you remember them.

7. Your mind can have a tendency to wander, causing you to lose track of the time. As with each **Mind Power Exercise**, you may set an alarm if you want to stop by a certain time. The *alpha* state is so pleasant for many that time can easily expand or contract, depending on your perception and thoughts. Clients frequently find themselves drifting on into the *theta* state while doing self-hypnosis. If you find yourself with a tendency to go to sleep, you may find it helpful to actually open your eyes and read your affirmations a second time if you feel your mind starting to drift and wander. Then close them again and day-dream your goal as explained above.

8. Bring yourself back to full *beta* awareness when ready by counting from one to five and opening your eyes.

9. Now that you have a *key word, use it!* Put a 3x5 card with your key word on it in a location where you will see it several times daily. My wife and I both have cards on the bathroom mirror with our

key words. Mine is in capital letters, contained in one of my favorite affirmations. The rest of the affirmation is in lower case letters so that the key word stands out.

Tips for Success

Do **Mind Power Exercise** IV regularly until you find yourself automatically motivated to reach your goal—then use the same tools to help reach other important goals. You will find that your ability improves with practice, just as muscles strengthen with physical exercise.

You may wish to use your own voice to record your affirmations for playback during your **Mind Power Exercise**. If so, you should state them clearly and slowly into the recorder in the *second person* (such as, "You are calm, confident, and in control of your emotions") so that your subconscious hears them as hypnotic suggestions. You can even include your own induction and wake-up instructions if desired, as long as they are also recorded in the second-person format.

Remember the five methods of subconscious programming and look for possible ways to incorporate them. It's very important, however, while using *any* subconscious programming tool other than repetition, to *monitor what is going into your mind*. You must guard your thoughts at these times. If you do not monitor out the garbage, you may still find yourself manipulated by others.

Also, by *being aware* of when your subconscious is open and vulnerable, you have a much greater opportunity to really take control of your life.

Conclusion

Hypnosis is very important in facilitating changes at a subconscious level, but it should be clear by now that hypnosis is not a panacea.

I strongly believe hypnosis has a valid place in the world today for all who are interested in self-improvement. In my opinion, it's equally important for us to be aware of the other ways of getting into the subconscious— not only to make desirable changes in our lives, but also to take more control over our own lives by monitoring out negative input.

People frequently ask me questions about hypnosis, so I have listed some of the most often asked questions and my answers in Appendix I.

In closing, let me repeat that you cannot force your subconscious to accept anything, any more than a high pressure salesperson can force you to buy. You must *allow* your subconscious mind to be persuaded to accept the desired changes by getting involved in the *benefits*. It has been my intention in this book to show you *how*. Rather than worrying about the price of change, focus on the *benefits of success*.

I believe it's time we learn how to make our subconscious minds become our servants rather than our masters. Now *you* have the tools— the rest is up to you.

May all your good dreams in life become success - ful realities— through **Mind Power Exercise.**

Session Four
Review

A.   Designing Effective Affirmations

1.   Affirmations are intended to help you put positive ideas into your _____ .
2.   You get what you believe, so properly constructed affirmations can help you change your beliefs.
3.   Since affirmations resemble hypnotic suggestions, _____ is vitally important.
4.   Write them down!

B.   Edit Your Affirmations

Refer to the examples until you feel you have sufficient understanding of the basics.

C.   Choose a Key Word

1.   This is used to represent your affirmations at a subconscious level.
2.   Your key word must feel good emotionally and intellectually.
3.   Write it down! Indicate that whenever you say, hear, see, or think your word that it _____ all of your affirmations.

D.   *Mind Power Exercise IV*

1.   Read your affirmations and focus on your key word.
2.   Enter self-hypnosis.
3.   Say or think your key word.
4.   Daydream reaching your goal, fantasizing your emotional satisfaction of success.

5. Use your key word in the waking state to reinforce the entire program and help facilitate your success!

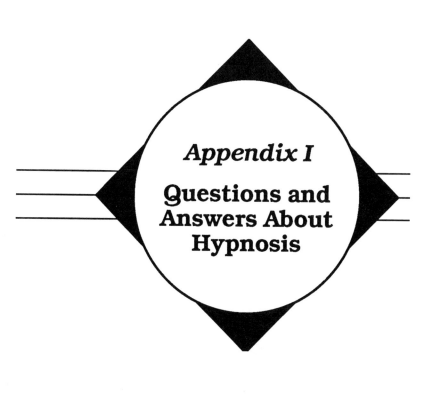

Appendix I

Questions and Answers About Hypnosis

Appendix I

Q. What is the best time of day for *Mind Power Exercise?*

A. This varies from person to person. For me, the best time is in the afternoon. Some people obtain maximum benefit in the early morning, while others find an evening time better. Experiment with various times until you find what works best for you.

Q. Should I turn out the lights when I do self-hypnosis?

A. This is a matter of personal preference. Some people are greatly distracted by light, particularly if it is bright, as images can sometimes be seen on the eyelids. Some people prefer total darkness. I personally am very comfortable with soft lighting.

Q. If I learn self-hypnosis, why would I ever need to go to a hypnotherapist?

A. Using self-hypnosis is like using mental muscles. Some changes require only easy "lifting" and you can make them without any help. Other changes require removing a mental "block" and can be facilitated by someone else helping or guiding you. If I move a chair alone, it's easy. If I have to move a piano, I need someone else on the other end to help lift. I have exchanged hypnosis sessions more than once with other hypnotherapists.

Q. If I go to a hypnotherapist, how can I be sure to choose one who is qualified and competent?

A. You can write for the names of one or more hypnotists in your area who are certified by the American Council of Hypnotist Examiners. (See page 98.)

Most competent hypnotists have completed some formal training in hypnotherapy— such as the 150-hour training program recommended by the American Council of Hypnotist Examiners. However, a certificate on the wall does not guarantee results in *any* profession, nor do academic credentials guarantee ethics. Ask for references. You might also choose to meet the hypnotist before agreeing to sessions.

Be aware that you should *not* ask a hypnotist to help you with a medical problem— such as relief from headaches— unless you have written consent from your physician. Hypnotists are not licensed to diagnose or treat illness unless also licensed as a physician.

Q. **Someone went to a 16-hour seminar to become a hypnotherapist. Doesn't it take longer to properly learn hypnotherapy?**

A. The American Council of Hypnotist Examiners recognizes the importance of supervised practice as well as training. A *minimum* of 150 hours of classroom instruction is recommended before private hypnotherapy should be attempted— although some supervised students are competent enough to do basic motivation and "stop smoking" sessions while in training.

In the "short cut" programs that some so-called specialists offer, one can learn a few basics— but in the long run may end up short-cutting clients. It's easy to learn how to hypnotize someone, but knowing how to guide them to successfully reach a goal requires more than experimenting with a few techniques learned over the course of a weekend.

I believe we can keep the level of professionalism high and well-respected if those wishing to learn hypnotherapy will seek out a qualified school rather than a travelling classroom/seminar held in a hotel.

For further information on training programs in your area and/or referral to a Certified Hypno-therapist, write to:

American Council of Hypnotist Examiners
1147 E. Broadway, Suite 340
Glendale, CA 91205
Telephone: 818-247-9379

Q. **You said there are five ways into the subconscious, but I've heard that people can be brainwashed by confusion. Couldn't this be considered a sixth method of subconscious programming?**
A. Confusing data tends to affect both the emotion and the conscious intellect, so in a sense could be a combination of emotion and alpha.

The use of confusing or conflicting input can be one of many methods of inducing hypnosis, as the conscious intellect can be so busy trying to sort out data that new conflicting data does not have time to get sorted. The result is that the "critical facility" is bypassed, and the individual goes into an alpha state.

Going into boot camp can be a very emotional experience for a young person who suddenly finds that *they mean business*. This could be in conflict with previous ideas or behavior patterns that used to work. As a result, someone who might have had great difficulty respecting authority may gain a new respect in a very short time.

Although some could choose to consider confusion as a separate method, I would consider it emotion and/or alpha, depending on the circumstances.

Q. **How did you get interested in hypnosis?**

A. When I was a highly stressed-out sales manager for a major corporation, I went to a hypnotherapist for stress management. I learned the simple stress coping technique described in **Mind Power Exercise** II and it changed my life. Although there have been times when I have not used it as well as I could and should, there have been other times when the coping technique has helped keep me from buying into stress levels that would have been very dangerous to my physical and mental health. Now, in my early forties, I feel and look younger than I did at 35.

This has made me appreciate the benefits of hypnosis.

Q. **What made you start doing hypnosis professionally, and where do you expect to go from here?**

A. Because of my growing interest, I began reading about hypnosis and related subjects. Eventually, I began practicing quite frequently on an amateur basis for friends, and found that I seemed to have a natural talent or skill at hypnosis.

My wife was very supportive of my interest and abilities and encouraged me to obtain formal training—which I did through a school certified by the American Council of Hypnotist Examiners. I went into hypnotherapy full time in early 1983, working at a clinic in downtown Seattle. Within a few months I went into business for myself.

My partner and I later incorporated with several other hypnosis clinics around the Puget Sound area to combine our resources for advertising, with the additional goal of raising the level of professionalism of what we do.

As to where we are going from here, time will tell. We certainly have personal and corporate goals. But our basic belief is to provide a quality service with a *win/win* philosophy.

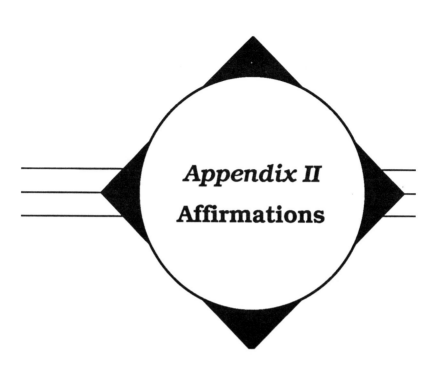

Appendix II
Affirmations

Affirmations for
Confidence

1. Each day I go through my daily activities with a confident and controlled attitude. I am calm, relaxed, and self-confident.
2. With this self-image, it becomes easier to go through all my daily activities controlled, relaxed, and comfortable. I am enjoying increasing confidence and success. I enjoy peace, health, and happiness in all my endeavors.
3. Should I desire extra strength or confidence, all I do is take a deep breath. As I exhale, the strength comes to be at my best in any situation.
4. Each day all things work to my advantage.
5. I do my **Mind Power Exercise** faithfully every day. Each time, I develop a sense of calm well-being, knowing that I am confident and competent in all situations.
6. I am an expert in my profession. I handle all areas of my profession easily and confidently. The many and varied situations in which I find myself are always handled competently in a calm, relaxed manner. I do all things well.
7. My personal time is always refreshing. I enjoy myself. I am always at my best no matter what the situation. I look good, my conversation is natural and easy, and my confident attitude attracts success. I always act, feel, and think as my self-image.
8. Each night, when I wish, I fall into a deep, restful, and peaceful sleep. When I awake at my desired time, I am happy, healthy, and completely refreshed, ready for new activity.
9. My confidence grows daily. I am now and shall ever remain as this self-image.
10. I take responsibility for being the person I choose to be, and I allow my desire to be my reality.

Recommended cassette tape:
#101 "Self-Confidence and Self-Image Programming

Appendix II

Affirmations for
Success

1. I am increasingly poised and confident in all situations. I know that my successful self-image improves and matures each day.
2. Each day I am influenced by those things that benefit me and my objectives. My activities add to my health, my strength, my energy, my prosperity, and my peace of mind. Each day in every way I get better and better and closer to my ideal self-image. I fulfill this image.
3. I am happy and healthy. I look good, my conversation is natural and easy, and my confident attitude attracts success.
4. I have my life plan well-defined and organized. My priorities and objectives are clear. I work with determination to see that my desires become reality. I control my own destiny.
5. Each day my relations with people become more pleasing and effective. I talk to people easily and naturally on first acquaintance and I initiate the conversation. I expect to do this. Any time I take a deep breath and think of this expectation, it gains strength and permanence.
6. I do my **Mind Power Exercise** faithfully every day so my self-image becomes more and more constructive in my life plan.
7. I see what others call problems as opportunities for growth and know that the best answers present themselves to me in deep states of relaxation.
8. I am worthy of my success. I accept my success naturally and gracefully.
9. My success continues to grow daily.
10. I take responsibility for being the person I choose to be, and I allow my desire to be my reality.

Recommended cassette tape:
#104 "Secrets of Success Attitudes"

Affirmations for
Stress Management

1. I am calm, relaxed, and self-confident. I think of myself this way. It is easy to be efficient and effective and still be calm and composed.
2. I picture myself as this new self-image, going through all my daily activities—both now and in the future—controlled, relaxed, and comfortable in all situations.
3. Each time I retire, I fall into a deep, restful, and peaceful sleep. When I awaken at my desired time, I feel happy and healthy, completely refreshed and ready for new activity.
4. When something happens that used to cause tension or stress, I take a deep breath and feel controlled and relaxed physically, mentally, and emotionally. As I exhale, I simply think the word "relax" and immediately feel relaxed— physically, mentally, and emotionally.
5. I do my **Mind Power Exercise** faithfully every day. Each time, I develop an increasing sense of serenity and calm well-being. I am now and shall remain as my new self-image.
6. When I wish to sleep, I take several deep breaths and think the words "relax and sleep" and easily drift into deep slumber.
7. Each day in every way I am more relaxed, calm, and composed.
8. I take responsibility for being the person I choose to be, and I allow my desire to be my reality.

Recommended cassette tape:
#103 "Deep Relaxation and Restful Slumber"

Affirmations for
Successful Telemarketing

1. I am a calm and confident person.
2. It becomes easier every day for me to communicate with people by telephone.
3. I am friendly over the phone and attract courtesy. If someone else chooses to be rude, I wish him or her a pleasant day and continue with my next call, remaining friendly.
4. Because I am friendly, it is easy to be calm and communicate with people. I like my new self-image and people like me.
5. I do my **Mind Power Exercise** faithfully every day, and my new self-image grows daily.
6. Because I like my new self-image, it is easy to be friendly. Other people enjoy talking with me, and they are also friendly.
7. My desire to use the telephone increases daily. It is a very quick and efficient way to find friendly prospects who are interested in my services.
8. I find it easier every day to determine quickly whether someone is a prospect for my services.
9. Every day in every way I find it easier and easier to equal or exceed my telemarketing goals. I set realistic goals for telemarketing. My mind remains focused on my successes.
10. I take responsibility for being the person I choose to be, and I allow my desire to be my reality.

Recommended cassette tape:
#118 "The Common Denominator of Success"

Affirmations for
Weight Control

1. I have a good attitude and believe in myself.
2. I desire to attain and maintain the best weight for my body because I am worth it.
3. As each day passes, the new slim, trim image of myself becomes more and more real. I always think, act, and move as this new self-image.
4. I enjoy eating the right foods in the right amounts. By eating more slowly, I am pleasantly satisfied from meal to meal.
5. Every day in every way I find it easier to do the things that help me reach and maintain my proper body weight.
6. I do my **Mind Power Exercise** faithfully every day, and my new self-image grows daily.
7. My self-control becomes stronger as I exercise it, just like a muscle becomes stronger with use.
8. My preference for the right foods increases with each passing day. I am satisfied after eating the appropriate amounts for my body. This satisfaction lasts from mealtime to mealtime.
9. As my new image becomes more and more real in my mind, it becomes more and more real in my body.
10. I take responsibility for being the person I choose to be, and I allow my desire to be my reality.

Recommended cassette tapes:
#105-A "Weight Control for Women"
#105-B "Weight Control for Men"

Affirmations for
Learning and Study Habits

1. I am calm, relaxed, and confident about my personal learning processes. I accomplish more in shorter periods of time and my work shows an increasing accuracy and understanding. This is my self-image.
2. When I read or hear material I wish to know and remember, I find I am able to recall all the important facts and details as I require them. My mind is always calm, relaxed, efficient, and orderly.
3. When I study I have the ability to concentrate for longer and longer periods of time as I wish, and to exclude all common distractions. My comprehension and recall improve daily.
4. When required, I have the ability to present this information quickly and easily, either orally, in written form, or by demonstration. I always communicate easily and effortlessly.
5. I do my **Mind Power Exercise** faithfully every day, and each time my self-image gains strength and maturity. My habits and attitudes reflect my confident self-image.
6. My memory improves daily.
7. Each day in every way it is easier to study, recall, and present information and to be in total self-control. I am now and shall remain as this self-image.
8. I take responsibility for being the person I choose to be, and I allow my desire to be my reality.

Recommended cassette tape:
#102 "Concentration—Perfect Memory and Recall"

Best Sellers!

TOTAL MIND POWER *by Donald L. Wilson, M.D.,*
Hypnotherapist
   How you can unlock the secrets to better health and happiness. Dr. Wilson's best-selling book teaches you easily learned, powerful techniques of Total Mind Power for tapping the other 90% of your mind.
Hardbound—Illustrated—254 pages $9.95

**SELF HYPNOSIS AND OTHER MIND EXPANDING TECH-
NIQUES** *by Charles Tebbetts, Hypnotherapist*
   New Enlarged Edition! Techniques and how-to of Self-Hypnosis, Autosuggestion, Behavior Modification, Faith Healing and Subconscious Reprogramming. Special sections on Weight Control and Stop Smoking.
Softbound—139 pages $5.95

THE LEARNING BLOCK *by Dean E. Grass, Hypnotherapist*
   A new technique for teaching through mind conditioning that works—teaches the student how to think and study more effectively; shows the teacher how to improve success with students; helps parents to understand what can be done to overcome the educational handicap of the slow learner.
Softbound—152 pages $6.95

HYPNOSPORT *by Les Cunningham*
   Why is it that a highly trained, superbly conditioned athlete's performance will fluctuate from one contest to another? This book answers that question by demonstrating the importance of mental training with hypnosis for improved athletic performance and consistency.
Softbound—180 pages $6.95

HYPNOSIS AND THE LAW *by Dr. Bradley Khuns, F.I.A.H.*
   A training manual in Forensic/Investigative Hypnosis (the use of "trance" in law enforcement and legal practice), based on actual findings, research, and the experiences of the author.
Hardbound—219 pages—Special! $11.95

HYPNOTISM AND THE MYSTICISM OF INDIA *by Ormond
McGill*
   Now you can learn Oriental Hypnotism as performed by the Masters of India—these are their secret teachings. Famed author and hypnotist Ormond McGill reveals how the real mysticism and magic of India is accomplished. You are taught how to become an adept.
Fully Illustrated—203 pages $12.50

UNLOCK YOUR MIND AND BE FREE WITH HYPNO-THERAPY *by Edgar A. Barnett, M.D.*
Dr. Barnett demonstrates the use of hypnotic age regression in which the patient's subconscious mind seeks out the traumatic emotional experiences which are directly responsible for their present symptoms and problems.
Softbound—155 pages $8.95

PROFESSIONAL STAGE HYPNOTISM *by Ormond McGill*
Covers all aspects of entertaining with hypnotism and explains the innermost secrets of stage hypnotism. Includes showmanship, presentation, staging, securing subjects, and dozens of thrilling routines.
Hardbound—203 pages $20.00

Best Seller!
SELECTIVE AWARENESS

By Peter Mutke, M.D.

Dr. Mutke gained an international reputation for his original research into breast development with hypnosis. Complete instructions for controlling headaches, muscle spasms, influencing circulatory system, weight reduction, self-image and breast development, improving sports performance and learning, and healing after surgery.

GIL BOYNE — Peter Mutke's brilliant structuring of a new view of self-therapy through self-hypnosis and self-programming gives specific instructions for:
1. Learning to deal with headaches, muscle spasms and other pains
2. Influencing your circulatory system
3. Directing weight reduction
4. Overcoming smoking
5. Self-image and breast development
6. Learning how to learn — how to take tests
7. Overcoming insomnia
8. Improving sports performance
9. Healing after surgery

Formerly a professor at John F. Kennedy University in California, Peter Mutke, M.D. now teaches "Selective Awareness Therapy" at the University of Berlin in West Berlin. This book has been translated into German and is the textbook for his course.

Softbound—195 pages—$7.95

HYPNOTHERAPY

The book that became a legend in just ten years!

By Dave Elman

Here's what the experts say:

DAVID CHEEK, M.D. – "Elman, like Quimby, Coue and LeCron, was a healer who developed his own credentials as an authority on hypnotism. *Hypnotherapy* is a most useful and practical summation of the teaching and thinking of a great humanitarian."

THEODORE X. BARBER, Ph.D. – "I had often heard of Elman's book but never found a copy. Westwood Publishing Co. has performed a valuable service in reprinting it."

WILLIAM J. BRYAN, JR., M.D. – Director, American Institute of Hypnosis – "As a teacher of hypnoanalysis, Dave Elman is without equal."

NATHANIEL BRANDON, Ph.D. – "I have never seen anyone induce a trance so quickly and anaesthesia so easily."

GIL BOYNE – Director, Hypnotism Training Institute – "In this major work, Elman strips away the academic verbiage and creates a forceful and dynamic presentation of hypnosis as a lightning-fast and amazingly effective tool in a wide range of therapies."

Hardbound—336 pages—$24.00

HYPNOSIS
and
POWER LEARNING

By Pierre Clement, Hypnotherapist

GIL BOYNE – This book undoubtedly contains the most efficient method ever published for acquiring self-hypnosis. The instructions are clear, simple and easy to follow, and ideally graduated. They are grounded on conditioned reflexes solidly anchored in every human being.

It is especially rich in methods of giving oneself post-hypnotic suggestions that "work." Some of them are "classics" for the practicing professional hypnotist. They are presented as "proofs-to-myself" of my "now-being-in-hypnosis." At the same time, they constitute a step-by-step training towards the USING of self-hypnosis; time self-hypnosis, deepening techniques, hand levitation, anesthesia, time distortion, multiple ways of developing a creative visualization . . . are just a few of them.

In the third part, the author comes to grips with the MIND POWER Learning methods. Supercharging your will power, concentration strengthening, memory activation (to the point of a photographic memory), increased speed of reading, maximized retention and recall "on the spur of the need of the moment" . . . are powerfully treated for application to yourself, NOW.

Softbound—138 pages—$7.95

HYPNOSIS:
New Tool in Nursing Practice

Edited by Gil Boyne

GIL BOYNE

In this first-of-its-kind textbook, I have collected the writings of a number of registered nurses who have used hypnotism in a great variety of special situations in medical settings. Among more than four thousand persons I have trained in hypnotherapy, there has been an increasing number of nurses who seem to intuitively grasp the central realization that hypnotism is the original and most effective "placebo effect."

The registered nurse is a "natural" hypnotist with a special capacity to use hypnotism creatively with hospital patients. It is the nurse who provides comfort and reassurance, administers pain-deadening medications and allays the patient's anxieties. There are at least three major reasons why the nurse is ideally suited to use hypnosis in patient care.

1. The patient's on-going, primary contact is with the nurse. Physician-patient contact is usually brief in duration and content.

2. Hospitalized patients often develop powerful feelings of helplessness and dependency which can trigger regression to a childlike ego-state. When this happens, the authority of the nurse is greatly magnified and the patient becomes highly responsive to suggestion, direction and instruction.

3. Because most nurses are female, they are often perceived by the patient as a mother surrogate, since it was mother who tended their needs and cared for them when they were sick as children.

The writers in this anthology have bypassed the technical writings of theoretic and experimental investigations, and have devoted themselves to addressing patients' problems with pragmatic methods based on therapeutic response.

The rapid changes in medical practice, the tremendous escalation of hospital costs, and the heavy demand on the physician's time have brought us to the realization that nurses must be given greater responsibility in the therapeutic treatment process rather than being restricted to the role of dispensers of comfort and medicine. It is my conviction that nurses are about to assume a new dimension in health care, gaining recognition as vital forces in the healing process.

Hardbound — 197 pages — $20.00

Best Seller!
HYPNOTISM
& MEDITATION

By Ormond McGill
Certified Hypnotherapist and Author of:
Professional Stage Hypnotism, The Hypnotism and Mysticism of India, How to Produce Miracles, etc.

Interest in both hypnotism and meditation is sweeping the world, but this is the first book that has ever been written that combines the two in a single process. They can be dovetailed into one. In *hypnomeditation,* self-hypnosis and meditation are skillfully blended, and the resulting techniques may be easily applied by persons in all walks of life to meet life with a new awareness and joyousness.

Hypnotism and Meditation is the operational manual for hypnomeditation. It opens new vistas for the hypnotist. Every process is clearly explained so you can put these techniques to work with both yourself and your subjects. **Detailed hypnomeditation formulas are given.** The results of the processes presented in this book are revolutionary. **Fifteen days with hypnomeditation will transform your life.**

Contents in fourteen comprehensive chapters cover: Understanding Hypnosis and Self-Hypnosis; The Power of Suggestion; The Hypnotic State of Mind; Preparing For Successful Conscious Self-Hypnosis; The Technique of Conscious Self-Hypnosis; Self-Hypnosis and Hypnomeditation; Understanding Meditation; Creating Your Inner Space; Techniques of Meditation; The Practice of Hypnomeditation; The White Light of Protection; The Source of Cosmic Power; Preparing for Hypnomeditation; Fifteen Days to Enlightenment; How To Effectively Use This Manual.

Softbound—99 pages—$5.95

Cassette Tape—Hypnomeditation by McGill
Includes 5 Daily Meditations—$7.95
SPECIAL—Book & Cassette—$11.95

You Can Activate the Power of Your Subconscious Mind and ... **COME ALIVE!**
with SELF HYPNOSIS and "POWER PROGRAMMING"
by Gil Boyne
Authority on Hypnosis Motivation and Mental Programming

SPECIAL OFFER! ANY 3 CASSETTES - $25 ANY 6 CASSETTES - $45

CASSETTE TAPE #101—SELF-CONFIDENCE THROUGH SELF-IMAGE PROGRAMMING
Radiate dynamic self-confidence—Improve your self-image—Overcome the fear of criticism, fear of rejection, fear of failure—Feel more lovable and appreciate yourself more. **$9.95**

CASSETTE TAPE #102—CONCENTRATION—MEMORY—RETENTION—PERFECT RECALL
This method is the only scientifically-validated memory system known—requires no memorization of key words or word associations—liberate your photographic memory—a fool-proof cure for forgetfulness—use your automatic mind search and memory-scanning capacity. The unique methods are placed indelibly into your subconscious mind for your permanent use. **$9.95**

CASSETTE TAPE #103—DEEP RELAXATION AND RESTFUL SLUMBER
Here is a new way to go to sleep! This incredibly effective and totally safe technique enables you to shed the cares of the day and drift off within minutes after your head hits the pillow. You float into a sleep as refreshing and rejuvenating as it is deep. You feel new vitality and energy each morning, and you maintain high energy levels through the day. **$9.95**

CASSETTE TAPE #104—SECRETS OF SUCCESS ATTITUDES
Overcomes your subconscious "will to fail"—you can learn to move rapidly toward your career and financial goals—success and riches spring from a foundation of "subconscious mental expectancy"—money does not come from high IQ, education, hard work or goodness—begin now to realize the enduring success and wealth that is potentially yours! **$9.95**

CASSETTE TAPE #105—TRIM AND FIT—WEIGHT CONTROL
The mental factors in compulsive overeating are widely recognized. This new method conditions your nervous system and your subconscious mind to rapidly move you toward your goal of attractive fitness. Gives you a new self-image about your physical self. Changes your eating habits by changing your appetite desires. Improves your figure easily and quickly. **$9.95**

CASSETTE TAPE #106—SECRETS OF COMMUNICATION AND EXPRESSION
How to present your ideas in a way that insures acceptance. If you are the one who feels fear and tension at the thought of having to give a speech or a short report, this tape is a blessing! You can speak with absolute confidence and perfect poise, whether to an audience of hundreds or a small group or a single person. **$9.95**

CASSETTE TAPE #107—DYNAMICS OF CREATIVE ACTING
Program your mind for success in your acting career. Covers auditions, rehearsing, performing, mental attitude and self-image. Overcome "The Freeze," learn lines quickly and easily. Express your creativity. **$9.95**

CASSETTE TAPE #108—DYNAMICS OF SELF-DISCOVERY
Answers the question, "WHO AM I?"! Overcomes the identity crisis. Creates a powerful belief in your own abilities. Discover the real self and your true capacity for joyful living! Teaches you how to give yourself—love, acceptance and approval. **$9.95**

CASSETTE TAPE #109—DYNAMIC HEALTH AND RADIANT VITALITY
You can overcome fears and negative beliefs and your state of health. This program subconsciously develops the mental imagery, feeling tone, and mental expectancy for radiant, vibrant expression of perfect health. **$9.95**

CASSETTE TAPE #110—SECRETS OF WINNING TENNIS—BEATING BETTER PLAYERS
NARRATED BY GIL BOYNE
Post-hypnotic suggestions and programmed mental images developed by a highly-ranked tennis pro now playing in professional competition. Improves your game within days! **$9.95**

CASSETTE TAPE #112—DYNAMICS OF CREATIVE WRITING
The hypnotic programming tape that was developed for a producer-writer of a famous dramatic-comedy T.V. show. This writer later claimed that this programming was an important factor in the creation of a script that won an Emmy nomination. **$9.95**

CASSETTE TAPE #114—YOU CAN STOP SMOKING NOW!
This power-programmed cassette will overcome the helpless feeling that underlies tobacco addiction. In just a short time, you become free of tobacco—permanently! Enjoy a longer, healthier, happier life. **$9.95**

CASSETTE TAPE #115—SEXUAL ENRICHMENT FOR MEN
You have the right to sexual happiness! Powerful desire, total function, and glowing fulfillment is the result of your use of this program. **$9.95**

CASSETTE TAPE #116—SEXUAL ENRICHMENT FOR WOMEN
A major breakthrough in sexual therapy. Teaches you how to be all that you can be. **$9.95**

CASSETTE TAPE #117—PROGRAMMING FOR THE HYPNOTHERAPIST!
Created exclusively for the Hypnotherapist, this program instills powerful confidence in one's ability to use hypnosis creatively, and to build a successful practice. **$9.95**

WESTWOOD PUBLISHING CO.
FILL IN AND MAIL . . . TODAY!

312 Riverdale Drive, Dept. MP65, Glendale CA 91204 (818) 242-3497

DESCRIPTION	PRICE	QTY	TOTAL
Total Mind Power	$ 9.95		
New Edition! Self Hypnosis	$ 5.95		
The Learning Block	$ 6.95		
Hypnosport	$ 6.95		
Hypnosis And The Law—Special!	$11.95		
Hypnotism & Mysticism of India	$12.50		
Unlock Your Mind And Be Free	$ 8.95		
Professional Stage Hypnotism	$20.00		
Selective Awareness	$ 7.95		
Hynotherapy	$24.00		
Hypnosis and Power Learning	$ 7.95		
Hypnosis: New Tool In Nursing	$20.00		
Hypnosis & Meditation	$ 5.95		
Hypnomeditation Cassette	$ 7.95		
SPECIAL—Hypnosis & Meditation, book and cassette	$11.95	1	1 95
Gil Boyne Programming Cassette Tapes (fill in item #) *104*	$ 9.95	9	95
SPECIAL OFFER—Any three cassettes in the Gil Boyne series	$25.00		
VERY SPECIAL OFFER!—Any six cassettes in the Gil Boyne series	$45.00		

POSTAGE & HANDLING			
up to $25 add $1.75 $26 to $60 add $2.75 $61 and above add $4.00	**TOTAL AMOUNT**	21. 90	
	POSTAGE AND HANDLING	1. 75	
	6.5% SALES TAX—L.A. COUNTY		
	6% SALES TAX—CALIF. ONLY		
	GRAND TOTAL	23. 65	

PRINT CLEARLY *CABBIE GLASS*

NAME *12455 SE 25TH ST.*

COMPANY OR BUSINESS NAME *Ms. G's Soft Works*

ADDRESS *12455 SE 25TH ST.*

CITY *BELLEVUE, WASH.*   ZIP *98055*

PHONE (AREA CODE) *(206) 641-5052*

SIGNATURE X *Carolyn Glass*

Note: Your order cannot be processed without a signature

☐ **Enclosed is my check payable to GIL BOYNE**

☐ **CHARGE MY: Bankamericard/Visa Mastercard (circle one)**

Credit Card No.																

		Mastercharge Inter Bank N. (above your name)	Expiration date required	Mo.	Yr.

USE YOUR CREDIT CARD . . . CHARGE BY PHONE
CALL ORDER DESK AT (818) 242-3497

"Hypnotism As A Career"

Learn to be a "People-Helper" — no college background required.

- Training In Clinical Hypnosis and Hypnotherapy
  - Accelerated/Intensives or Weekend Classes
- Diplomas awarded as "Master Hypnotist" and "Hypnotherapist"
  - Diplomas authorized by the Board of Education
  - Approved by the Superintendent of Public Instruction

For a catalog and a list of approved schools, write to
American Council of Hypnotist Examiners
1147 E. Broadway #340
Glendale, CA 91204

NOTES

NOTES

NOTES

NOTES

NOTES

NOTES

NOTES